RIDE GUIDE

MOUNTAIN BIKING IN THE NEW YORK METRO AREA

THIRD EDITION

BY JOEL D. SENDEK

Ecopress
An Imprint of Finney Company

Notice to the Reader

The information and material in this manual are accurate and true to the best of our knowledge. All recommendations are made without guarantee on the part of Anacus Press, Ecopress, or the author. The publishers and author disclaim any liability in connection with the use of information contained in this book or the application of such information.

The publisher advises the reader to consult and carry current local maps for the areas in which he/she is traveling to supplement the material within this book. Road conditions and other critical information provided in these pages will change. It remains the responsibility of the reader to have a thorough understanding of the routes, the condition of the bicycle, and his/her riding ability. By following the instructions contained herein, the reader willingly assumes all risks in connection with such instructions.

Ecopress
An Imprint of Finney Company
8075 215th Street West
Lakeville, Minnesota 55044
(952) 469-6699
www.finneyco.com

Third Edition
Previous editions published by Urban Country Publishers and Anacus Press 1995 and 1998

Allaire State Park, Cheesequake State Park, Hartshorne Woods Park, Henry Hudson Trail, Huber Woods Park, Ringwood State Park, Washington Valley Park, and Wawayanda State Park rides used with permission from *Ride Guide: New Jersey Mountain Biking*, Third Edition, Copyright 2008 Joshua M. Pierce.

ISBN 13: 978-0-933855-26-7
ISBN 10: 0-933855-26-5

Designed by Angela Wix
Edited by Lindsey Cunneen
Cover image by William Schmitt
Unless otherwise noted, all photography by Joel D. Sendek
Cartography by Moore Creative Designs

Printed in the United States of America
3 5 7 9 10 8 6 4

ACKNOWLEDGMENTS

To
my daughter Charlotte, who learned to ride a bike at 5
my son Jack, who learned to ride a bike at 4,
my son Jason, who is learning to ride now at 3,
and my wife Jenny, who kisses our boo-boos when we fall.

Charlotte, Jack, and Jason Sendek (clockwise from top).

CONTENTS

INTRODUCTION

RIDES IN NEW YORK CITY, NEW YORK

RIDES IN WESTCHESTER COUNTY, NEW YORK

RIDES IN PUTNAM COUNTY, NEW YORK

RIDES IN LONG ISLAND

RIDES IN CONNECTICUT

RIDES IN NEW JERSEY

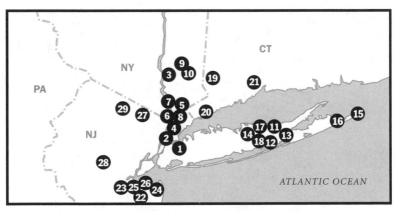

Numbers on map correspond to rides listed in the table of contents.

Curving among big trees in Connecticut.

FOREWORD

It has been at least a decade since I reviewed Joel Sendek's first edition of *Ride Guide: Mountain Biking in the New York Metro Area*. Much has changed since then. As of the spring of 2007, there is finally a place (albeit a small one) on the island of Manhattan where off-road riding won't earn you an expensive ticket. The irony is that there are probably more mountain bikers per square foot in the New York Metro Area than in all of the so-called mountain bike meccas (Moab, Crested Butte, Fruita, etc.) combined. When Joel wrote the first edition, it was a necessary tool for finding a place to ride. The third edition is a necessary tool, but now you need it to find all of the great trails that have been built in the interim. This is hardly a problem compared to the early days, and I must give Joel credit for helping the sport stay alive during that darker era.

As a former adventure travel writer, I've read my share of bad guidebooks. They range from the inaccurate to the uninformative to the incredibly dull. Joel's book is none of those, which is what made it stand out to me all those years ago. I sat down and read it cover to cover because it solved the puzzle of how to be a New York City mountain biker with the added bonus of just being a good read. You don't know me, but I'm not that easily amused. Just to frame my attention span for you: I got bored with adventure travel writing. That is, I got bored going on vacation on the company's tab. The book is good.

Basically, it comes down to this: If you are a New York City mountain biker and want to ride, you need to put your latte down and buy this book right now. And maybe I'll see you at Mianus River Park where I ride with my brother-in-law whenever I visit. It's great. And you're hearing that from a guy who has 25 miles of Vermont trails right outside his door every day.

Don Cuerdon, a.k.a. "Captain Dondo," *Mountain Bike Magazine*
December 2007

IMPORTANT DISCLAIMERS

Mountain Biking Can Be Dangerous

Mountain biking is an exciting but dangerous and physically demanding sport. The goal of this book is to provide information on destinations for the mountain biker. While there is a short discussion of riding techniques and tips, this is no substitute for professional training or guidance. In addition, there can be no assurance that the trails described in this book will be passable or free of dangers such as falling rocks and trees, overflowing streams, and wild animals. Serious injury or death may result from mountain biking on the trails described in this book. The author and the publisher will not be liable if such calamities occur to a reader of this book. All riders, regardless of skill level, should treat all trails with caution and respect by giving the necessary care to the local environment.

Land Use Rules/Landowners' Right to Privacy

This book contains information on existing trails which, at the time of printing, were accessible and to the best of the author's knowledge, open to mountain bikers and legal to ride. However, it is possible that any trail might be closed to mountain bikers at any time for reasons such as land ownership changes or environmental concerns. It is the rider's responsibility to heed signs warning against trail use. If it is evident that a certain trail or a part of a trail is off limits to mountain biking, please don't ride that trail, even if it is described in this guide. In addition, please respect landowner's rights to privacy by obeying any "no trespassing" or similar signs that you may encounter on your rides. These signs often appear near official mountain-biking trails because parkland is sometimes adjacent to private property.

Accuracy

This book was written using information that is believed to be accurate based on sources that are believed to be reliable. The publisher makes no assurance that the trail mileage markers or descriptions are accurate, as time and trail users may change the appearance of a trail.

USING THIS BOOK

The Mountain Biking Phenomenon

Congratulations! You are taking part in one of the fastest growing sports in the United States. More than 80 percent of the new bicycles bought in the United States in 2005 were mountain bikes. And every year, hundreds of new trails open up for the mountain bikers to enjoy.

Mountain Biking in the New York Area

Few people realize that some of the best mountain biking in the United States is located within a reasonable commute from midtown Manhattan. In fact, there are hundreds of trails in the New York metro area, many that seldom have more that a few visitors at one time. The trails in the New York area offer a range of difficulty suitable for any level of off-road cyclist, from beginner to advanced. The destinations described in this book were carefully selected to provide metropolitan area mountain bikers with the best trails at every level of difficulty, and most are open to mountain bikers year-round. Most of the trail descriptions in this book include information on all of the following:

> **Location:** This lists the town that is nearest to the trail.
>
> **Distance from New York City:** This is the approximate traveling time (with mileage) from midtown Manhattan to the trailhead, by train or car. In general, either mode of transportation takes about the same amount of time. In some cases train travel may take longer since you might have to ride a few miles from the train station to the trailhead. Regarding the drive time, typical New York City traffic is accounted for; however, during busy holiday weekend travel periods, allow extra time.
>
> **Trails Described:** This lists the trails included in this location.

Overview
This is a general summary of the area.

Directions by Car and Directions by Train
This includes complete, detailed directions from Manhattan to the trailhead via train or car.

Trip Length: This is the total round-trip distance of the ride, measured in miles. Be sure to allow enough time—and daylight—to complete your ride! Each trail was carefully measured and double-checked with a bike odometer for accuracy, though distances may vary somewhat.

Difficulty: This provides a rating measure of the technical difficulty of a given route description. The routes are rated beginner, intermediate, or advanced, according to the following rating system:

> **Beginner:** Relatively flat terrain; groomed trails or pavement with gentle hills.

> **Intermediate:** Rolling hills with some rough terrain and occasional surface obstacles.

> **Advanced:** Steep, tight, demanding trails with long hills and frequent obstacles.

These ratings reflect the mountain-biking skill level required to be able to ride a given route successfully. Naturally, you might find an occasional steep hill on a "beginner" trail or some flat sections on an "advanced" trail. Also, keep in mind that weather, trail conditions, and temperature may change the difficulty of a trail substantially and adjust accordingly when riding in excessively wet or hot conditions.

Trail Configuration: This is the description of the configuration of each trail. Loop, out-and-back, figure-eight, or combination. The description of an out-and-back will be one way (though the trail will look very different on the way home!). To get back, simply follow the route description in reverse.

Elevation Change: This is the difference in feet between the highest and lowest point on the trail. The greater the elevation change, the more strenuous a given ride is likely to be.

Trail Type: This is a description of the predominant type of terrain encountered on a given trail such as:

> **Singletrack:** A path wide enough for one bike only. These are often the best trails to ride.

> **Doubletrack:** A dual-track path with grass or rocks in between.

> **Carriage trail:** A rough, unpaved road or wide trail unsuitable for cars but traversable by four-wheel-drive vehicles.

> **Pavement:** Flat, paved trail.

🚲 *THE ROUTE*

This is a complete, detailed description of the ride, including mileage markers and intersections (sometimes noted as spur trails), stream crossings, landmarks, and other highlights of the trail. The first time you ride one of the trails described here, go slowly and follow the directions carefully to avoid getting lost and having to walk your bike through treacherous terrain. Each turn is important. The detailed routes described for each destination in this book are the result of many months of riding nearly every trail in each of the parks. While it was certainly enjoyable to explore all the accessible trails during the preparation of this book, if you want to ride only the very best trails, stick to the routes described here. Remember a few landmarks along the way, and soon you will have the routes memorized.

MAP INFORMATION

The trail format follows this system:

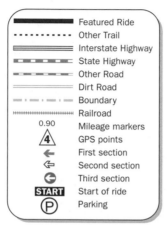

The specific directions of the routes for each park are set up as follows:

Pt. to
Point   **Cume**   **Turn**   **Landmark**

Pt. to Point: This indicates the distance in hundredths of a mile from the last turn or point of interest.

Cume: This is short for cumulative and is the total mileage from the starting point of the route.

Turn: The abbreviations in this column are:

L	Left
R	Right
S	Straight
BL	Bear Left
BR	Bear Right
X	Turn around, retrace trail
T	Intersection the trail ends at and you must go either right or left to continue.

Landmark: This includes descriptions along the trail for orientation.

A nice groomed trail in Long Island.

TRANSPORTATION TO THE TRAILS

Most of the trails described in this guide are within an hour's train or car ride from New York City and are suitable for day trips. A separate and complete set of directions for driving or commuter train travel is included for most destinations.

Commuter Train Lines

There are six train lines that service the trails described in this guide. These include the Metro North Hudson Line, the Metro North New Haven Line, the Metro North Harlem Line, the Long Island Railroad, New Jersey Transit, and the PATH Train. The three Metro North trains depart from Grand Central Station. The Long Island Railroad departs from Penn Station. The PATH train runs from Manhattan to the New Jersey Transit terminals in New Jersey. The PATH has six subway-type entrances, including four along 6th Avenue and at Christopher Street in Greenwich Village. Schedule information is available at any of the train stations or by calling the following numbers:

Metro North Trains: NYC (212) 532-4900; www.mta.info
Long Island Railroad: (718) 217-LIRR; www.mta.info
PATH: (800) 234-PATH; www.njnyrails.com
New Jersey Transit: NJ (800) 772-2222; www.njtransit.com

All trains require train-issued bike passes in order for cyclists to travel on the train with a bicycle, though no additional fare is necessary once you have a bike permit. The level of enforcement of these policies varies depending on the train's conductor, so to be safe, follow the rules and obtain a bike pass for any trains on which you intend to travel with your bicycle. The procedure for obtaining a pass for each train line and relevant restrictions are as follows:

Metro North Trains: Leave from Grand Central Station. A permit is required to travel with a bike and is available for $5 at Window 27 at Grand Central Terminal. You may also apply for your permit through the mail. Call (212) 340-2176 to request an application. The permit is good for life. Restrictions are as follows:

   • *Weekends and holidays:* No restrictions except during the following holidays, when no bikes are permitted: New Year's Eve, New Year's

Day, St. Patrick's Day, Mother's Day, Rosh Hashanah Eve, Thanksgiving Eve, Thanksgiving Day, Yom Kippur Eve, Christmas Eve, and Christmas Day. Also, no bikes are permitted on trains scheduled to depart Grand Central between 12 noon and 8:30 p.m. on the Friday before Memorial Day weekend, day or weekend before July 4th , and the Friday before Labor Day weekend.

- *Weekdays outbound from Grand Central:* No bikes between 7:00 and 9:00 a.m. and 3:01 and 8:15 p.m. On the Friday after Thanksgiving and the week between Christmas and New Year's, no bikes between 7:00 a.m. and 12 noon and 3:00 and 8:30 p.m.
- *Weekdays inbound to Grand Central:* No bikes between 6:00 and 10:00 a.m. and 4:00 and 7:00 p.m. On the Friday after Thanksgiving and the week between Christmas and New Year's, no bikes between 5:00 a.m. and 12 noon and 4:00 and 7:30 p.m.
- A maximum of 2 bicycles per car, 4 bicycles per train is allowed.
- You cannot ride your bike on the platform or restrict the mobility of other passengers.

Long Island Railroad: Leave from Penn Station. A permit is required to travel with a bike. Permit applications can be obtained by calling (718) 990-8228. The permit is good for life and costs $5. Restrictions are as follows:

- *Seasonal (Memorial Day – Labor Day) restrictions on weekends:*
  - o No bikes Saturdays and Sundays departing outbound from Penn Station between 7:30 and 10:00 a.m.
  - o No bikes Saturdays inbound to Penn Station arriving between 8:00 and 10:00 a.m. and 4:00 to 6:00 p.m.
  - o No bikes Sundays and Monday holidays inbound to Penn Station arriving between 4:00 and 6:00 p.m. and Montauk trains arriving 3:00 to 10:00 p.m.
- *Rest of year:*
  - o No restrictions on Saturdays.
  - o No bikes Sundays inbound to Penn Station from Montauk arriving between 6:30 and 10:00 p.m.
- *Holidays:* No bikes are permitted on the following holidays: New Year's Eve, New Year's Day, St. Patrick's Day, Mother's Day, Rosh Hashanah Eve, Columbus Day, Thanksgiving Eve, Thanksgiving Day, Yom Kippur Eve, Christmas Eve, and Christmas Day. Monday holidays: see seasonal section.
- *Weekdays outbound from Penn Station:* No bikes between 7:00 a.m.

and 9:00 a.m. and 3:00 and 8:00 p.m.
* *Weekdays inbound to Penn Station:* No bikes between 6:00 and 10:00 a.m. and 4:00 and 7:00 p.m. (6:00 and 7:00 p.m. from Montauk).
* A maximum of 2 bicycles per car and 4 bicycles per train is allowed.
* You cannot ride your bike on the platform of restrict the mobility of other passengers.

PATH: Leave from various points in Manhattan. No permit is required to board PATH trains with a bicycle. Restrictions are as follows:

* A maximum of 2 bicycles per car is allowed.
* You cannot ride your bike on the platform of restrict the mobility of other passengers.
* *Weekdays (non-holiday):* No bikes permitted between 6:00 and 9:30 a.m. and between 3:00 and 6:30 p.m.
* *Saturdays:* No bikes on Manhattan trains between 1:00 and 7:00 p.m.; no bikes traveling east from New Jersey between 7:00 a.m. and 2:00 p.m.

New Jersey Transit: Leave from various points in New Jersey, and connect with the PATH train in Hoboken. A permit is required to travel with a bike. Permit applications can be obtained at Penn Station or by calling (201) 491-9400. The permit is free and will be mailed to you. Restrictions are as follows:

* Full-size bicycles are permitted on the North Jersey Coast, Raritan Valley, Main/Bergen County, and Port Jervis lines only.
* Collapsible bicycles are permitted on all lines at all times.
* *Weekends and holidays:* No restrictions on weekends except for all major holidays, when no bikes are permitted. These holidays include New Year's Eve, New Year's Day, St. Patrick's Day, Rosh Hashanah Eve, Thanksgiving Day, the day after Thanksgiving Day, Yom Kippur Eve, Christmas Eve, and Christmas Day. Also, no bikes are permitted on Fridays before holiday weekends.
* *Weekdays:* No bikes between 5:00 and 9:30 a.m. and 4:00 and 7:00 p.m. Also, no bikes are permitted on Fridays before holiday weekends.
* Bicyclists must be at least 16 years old.
* Bicyclists must carry two 24-inch elastic bungee-type cords to secure bikes to the disabled-accessible areas of the train.
* Bicycles are allowed only on locomotive-hauled Comet rail equipment with disabled-accessible areas. A maximum of two bicycles per accessible area is permitted.

• Bicyclists may not ride on the platform, use escalators, or restrict the mobility of other passengers.

• NJ Transit personnel have the authority to restrict bicycle carriage due to overcrowded trains or unsafe conditions.

Note: Bikes are allowed on New York City subways, though it might be difficult to do so during rush hour.

When traveling on a train with your bike, it is best to keep it within view at all times, preferably in the seat in front of you. Occasionally, if the train is full, the conductor may suggest you leave your bike in an adjoining empty car or in between cars. This is generally safe also, because the conductor won't allow others to go into those cars. However, pay attention during station stops when passengers are entering and exiting near where your bike is stowed. For further piece of mind, lock your bike. Overall, despite the one-time hassle of obtaining a permit and becoming familiar with scheduling restrictions, traveling on a train with a bike is really quite easy. Since the train lines allow bikes as a public service at a nominal fee, be sure to be extra friendly to train personnel and other passengers so that New York cyclists will continue to have access to the train lines.

Driving

Drivers have the convenience of setting their own schedule and have no excuse for not popping their bikes in the trunk and heading to the trails every weekend. However, for those many New Yorkers who prefer to spend money on mountain-biking equipment instead of motor vehicles, car rentals are always an option. Hertz, Avis, and many other car rental companies have a number of rental locations in New York City. Be sure to call up to a week in advance for summer weekends to reserve a car, and allow even more time near holidays. Also, make sure to get a car in which the back seats fold down to allow room in which to transport your bike.

WHAT TO WEAR

Typical mountain-biking wear includes padded cycling shorts, a T-shirt or cycling jersey, cycling shoes or running shoes (depending on the pedal system the bike has), and cycling gloves. Many trails traverse streams and have muddy sections, so leave the tennis whites at home. The following suggestions are in order of importance:

Helmet

Wear a helmet. Most bicycle injuries can be prevented simply by wearing one. Be careful, though; an incorrectly fitting helmet may offer little protection, if any. Make sure the straps are tight against your chin and the helmet fits snugly. Looking in a mirror, you should not be able to see much of your forehead with a properly adjusted helmet. After the straps are fastened, try to slide the helmet off your head. If you can, take the helmet off and tighten the straps. Also, before your buy a helmet, check the label inside to make sure it meets either ANSI or Snell safety standards. Pay $60 to $100 and buy a quality helmet that fits well and looks good on you.

Shorts

Wear cycling shorts instead of regular shorts or tights because the seamless crotch lined with soft, absorbent padding will reduce friction between your body and the notoriously uncomfortable bicycle seats. Regular shorts tend to get caught up around the saddle. While bicycle shorts might feel funny at first (especially since they are designed to be worn without underwear), you'll get used to them quickly and be thankful you wore them at the end of your ride. For those who don't like the skin tight look of traditional cycling shorts, there is now a large selection of normal "baggy" looking shorts available with bicycle short-quality liners. Ask for them at your local bike shop. Bicycle short prices range from $20 for a basic cycling short to $80 for a top-of-the-line short.

Gloves

Cycling gloves have padded palms that help prevent hand blisters. They also protect your hands in a fall. In cold weather, wear full-fingered gloves. A decent pair of gloves costs $15. Winter gloves may be more pricey.

Shirt

A tight-fitting cycling jersey might at first seem superfluous but is worth considering because these garments are made to fit snugly in order to reduce wind resistance. The tight fit also helps avoid snagging branches on narrow trails. In addition, most cycling jerseys have pockets in the back which conveniently allow you to pack food, maps, keys, and other items safely, without interfering with your cycling motion. Jerseys start at about $25.

Shoes

Depending on the pedal system you have on your bike, an old pair of tennis shoes or light-weight hiking boots may be all you need. Stiff-soled mountain-biking shoes that clip in to pedals like ski boots into ski bindings will enhance power transmission. Bring along an extra pair of socks on a long ride so that you can change into them if your feet get wet while peddling through a puddle or stream. Quality mountain-biking shoes start at about $100/pair.

Pants

In cooler weather, wear tights over cycling shorts. It's better not to wear sweat pants or jeans, because these looser-fitting garments may get tangled up in your bicycle's drive train or snag of branches near the trails.

Glasses

This is a good idea to protect eyes from leaves, dirt and branches that might fly into your face as you are whizzing by, it is important to wear glassed even if the weather is overcast. Many manufacturers produce sunglass "kits" designed specifically for mountain bikers, with three interchangeable lenses in clear, amber, and black.

Body Armor

For more aggressive riders, a set of elbow, knee, and shin guards are a good investment to cushion inadvertent falls in the woods.

Winter Riding

Layer, layer, layer! In general wear less than you think you should, because the aerobic nature of cycling will warm you up quickly. Make sure that your first layer is lycra or other body-hugging material, and wear a wind breaker as your outer layer. A thin hat underneath your helmet or a head band that covers your ears is a good idea. You also might want to wear a neck gaiter to keep your neck warm and to breath through to warm up frigid air before it enters your mouth. Later in the ride if you start to overheat, simply peel off your top layer, leave it in a tree, and pick it up on your way back.

With the proper gear, you can comfortably ride most New York area trails year-round.

WHAT TO TAKE ALONG

Mountain Bike

No mountain bike adventure is complete without one. Buy the best bike you can afford and buy it at a bike store or sporting goods shop where you can get a test ride, professional assembly, a complete fitting, tune-ups, and other service later. Buying a bike at a warehouse club or discount store just isn't worth it. Plus, prices of name-brand, high performance bicycles—which are typically available only at bike shops—continue to fall, with entry-level mountain bikes starting around $250. Of course, some bikes still cost in excess of $5,000, but in general even full suspension bikes (i.e. a bike equipped with shock-absorbers) are available for reasonable prices.

Water

Water is essential to stay well hydrated while cycling in order to avoid fatigue. Either use bladder-type hydration system or make sure your bike is equipped with two water bottle cages. Try to drink a minimum of one bottle for every hour you are riding. Drink before you are thirsty. On longer rides, take extra water in a fanny pack or fill up at water fountains or service stations along the way. On cold days, start with warm water to prevent it from freezing. On hot days, leave your water bottle in the freezer before your ride.

Food

Take along energy bars or bananas to provide fuel to keep your legs moving. Eat before you are hungry. You can find energy bars at bicycle shops and health food stores. Contrary to popular belief, many energy bars actually taste good. While Powerbar remains the gold-standard energy bar, a personal favorite is Clif Bar, which offers great-tasting bars with innovative flavors such as apricot and cookies and cream.

Flat Repair Kit

You should be equipped to fix a flat tire if you are so unfortunate. This involves bringing along either a spare inner tube or a tube patch kit, tire levers to remove and replace the tire, and a pump. Make sure that you have a pump that fits the valve on your tires. Valves come in two varieties, Presta and Schrader. Schrader valves are the same as the valves on car tires. Presta valves are smaller. While pumps come in many different sizes, buy a mini-pump which is small enough to carry in a jersey pocket. The longer "frame-pumps" are easily jarred loose on rocky terrain. Always check your tires before a ride to make sure there is adequate tire pressure (around 35 psi). In general, inflate the tires to a higher pressure in the colder months or when riding on pavement or frozen ground. Tubeless tires are becoming more popular as they are filled with self-sealing liquid to guard against punctures. If you have this system, be sure to pack a tube just in case you have a major hole that requires a temporary tube to repair.

Seat Pack/Tool Kit
Attach this underneath the saddle to carry a flat repair kit, identification, credit cards, money, keys, and a multi-tool. These are light-weight, all-in-one tools that usually incorporate a screwdriver, chain tool, allen wrenches, spoke wrenches, and socket wrenches.

Cyclocomputer/Odometer
This is useful to have to follow the mileage markers in this guide, and it will also help keep track of your speed and how many miles you have ridden. Many varieties are available, and most cost $30 or less.

Bug Spray
Apply a generous amount of repellent before riding to ward off the annoying pesky insects that tend to hang out in the woods and "bug" humans who invade their territory. Choose one that contains Deet, which has been shown to repel ticks, and spray it on clothing as well as any exposed skin areas. Lyme Disease is common in suburban New York. It is a tick-borne illness that is caused by a corkscrew-shaped bacterium known as spirochete (*Borrelia burgdorferi*). The ticks that transmit Lyme Disease are about the size of a poppy seed. Some relevant information, according to recent research:

- Only a small percentage of ticks are infected with the bacteria that cause Lyme Disease.
- An infected tick must be attached to skin for 24 hours for disease transmission to occur.
- Lyme Disease is easily treatable with antibiotics if caught early.

The best way to avoid Lyme Disease is to wear clothing that covers the entire body and wash the clothes after every ride. On warmer days when wearing fewer clothes, inspect all exposed areas of skin for ticks after riding, scrub thoroughly. If you later notice the painless bull's-eye rash that indicates Lyme Disease, notify your doctor, who will invariably prescribe antibiotic therapy. For more information, look at the American Lyme Disease Foundation Web site at www.aldf.com.

Photo by William Schmitt

Scooting down a ladder in Connecticut.

MOUNTAIN BIKING ETIQUETTE

Rules of the Trail
At the risk of sounding like Miss Manners, there are some rules you should follow on the trail to help everyone enjoy the backcountry to the fullest extent. You will encounter hikers, equestrians, and wild animals that have all enjoyed mountain bike-free trails for decades. In order for us to continue to have access to trails, we must act responsibly and show respect to those who share the trails with us.

As a general guide, always observe the International Mountain Bicycling Association's "Rules of the Trail" (used with permission):
1. Ride on open trails only
2. Leave no trace
3. Control your bicycle
4. Always yield trail
5. Never spook animals
6. Plan ahead

Ride On Open Trails Only
If a trail is closed to bikes, don't ride that trail. While the trails in this book have been carefully selected to be legal for mountain bikers, respect trail closures if they occur, and if you see a "no bikes" or "no trespassing" sign, ride somewhere else. There are plenty of other trails to ride. Most importantly, the example you set will affect trail access for all cyclists. See Land Use Rules.

Leave No Trace
Stay on marked trails and don't attempt to make new ones, which could have a negative environmental impact. And of course, don't leave any wrappers or trash behind.

Control Your Bicycle
Don't ride at excessive speeds or you could seriously injure yourself or others.

Always Yield Trail

When encountering others, announce your approach well in advance. *Always* greet people on the trails. It is important to be friendly and courteous to maintain a positive image of the sport, which will ultimately result in continued or expanded trail access. When passing in the opposite direction, show respect for hikers by slowing down or stopping. Also, be careful when rounding corners or other blind spots.

Never Spook Animals

Animals may be frightened by sudden movements or unannounced approaches. Startling an animal may cause harm to the animal or to you. Remember, the forest is their living room. When you encounter an equestrian, stop, get off your bike, and allow the horse plenty of room to pass. The key here is communication. To be safe, ask the equestrian for instructions.

Plan Ahead

Keep your bike in good repair, bring food, water, and tools, and know where you are going and how to get back home. Know your ability and be self-sufficient. And of course, always wear a helmet.

Give Something Back!

In general, keep in mind that mountain biking on public land is a right, not a privilege. An excellent way to maintain this right and create new trail riding opportunities is to volunteer at a local park. Spending a few hours on trail maintenance or other useful programs generates tremendous goodwill toward mountain bikers. New Jersey, Long Island, New York City, and Westchester each have local mountain-biking clubs. Further information on these clubs can be found at www.climbonline.org (Long Island), www.nycmtb.com (New York City), and www.wmba.org (Westchester). Another good idea is to join a national mountain-biking association. A tax-deductible $20 membership to the International Mountain Bicycling Association (IMBA), for example, will support its broad-based effort to promote the sport and expand trail access for all riders. For membership information call IMBA at (303) 545-9011 or go to www.imba.com.

BASIC MOUNTAIN BIKING SKILLS

Riding Downhill

The most important technique for effective downhill riding is to shift your weight back. This means lifting your rear end off the saddle and angling it down toward the rear tire. In downhill races, some professionals look like they are *riding* on the back tire, but don't try doing this anytime soon (especially you guys out there who hope to become fathers someday). However, getting your butt back will help you avoid forward end-over-end somersaults (known as "endos") that are much more likely to occur when a rider's weight is not shifted back on a downhill. Also, look as far down the hill as possible—try for 10-20 feet. Have faith that your bike will pull you through the current terrain and spend time preparing to position yourself for that next rock garden or stream. It's just like driving—drivers that are constantly focused on the hood ornament are ill prepared to deal with upcoming action. When going straight, keep your pedal parallel to the ground (3 o'clock and 9 o'clock) to avoid catching obstacles in the trail. When cornering, bring your outside pedal down and lean in to the turn.

Braking

Most stopping power comes from the front brake. However, using the front brake alone may cause an endo, especially if your bike is equipped with powerful disc brakes. Beginners tend to use their brakes too much. The less you use your brakes, the more momentum you bike builds up and the more stability you have. In addition, a death grip on the brakes tenses your hands and fingers and causes fatigue throughout your entire body. In contrast, loose arms absorb hits and allow you to go faster and feel better—and not have to replace your brake pads so often!

Riding Uphill

The first thing to do before an upgrade is to downshift. By doing this you avoid peddling in too high of a gear and also avoid grinding the gears down while struggling up a rocky slope. In good trail conditions, climb in whatever position is most comfortable—either on the saddle or standing. Wider hand position provides better breathing and more power and control. In rainy, rocky, or loose trail conditions, the best technique is to remain in the saddle and keep most of your weight over the rear of the bicycle to maintain good traction by the back tire. Regardless of the trail condition, it is important to look ahead and plan a line of travel through the path of least resistance. In other words, choose a path that goes around the most intimidating rocks, logs, and other obstacles, and ignore them as you motor past. Finally, maintain a steady pedal stroke and think about slipping down the single track on the other side!

Traversing Logs and Other Obstacles

The key to taming logs and other obstacles successfully is not to overreact to them. An old cliché is quite appropriate here: Don't make a mountain out of a molehill. In other words, don't be intimidated. Gain confidence by biking over small sticks or small logs. Then get comfortable close to home riding directly over the curb from the street onto the sidewalk. To lighten the blow on the front tire, do a small wheelie to bring the front tire up over the curb. Lowering your torso over the bike will assist in performing this maneuver. Use the same technique on the trail. It's more of a challenge when the obstacle is in the middle of a climb. To maintain momentum, shift your whole body over the handlebars and toward the front of the bike after your front tire is on top of the obstacle. This reduces the weight on the back tire and makes it easier to bring it over the obstacle.

Getting Lost

The best way to avoid getting lost is to follow the routes described in this book. However, to allow for an occasional detour now and then to follow a turkey or seek out a waterfall, take the necessary precautions to make sure you can find your way back to the main trail. The best way to avoid getting lost is to make mental notes of things such as odd tree shapes, rock formations, any man-made structures or any kind of water on or near the trail. Traveling with a compass or GPS is also a good idea, especially in the winter months when it is more difficult to discern direction by noting sun position. Use your ears, also, to listen for cars. This is usually a tip-off that civilization is not too far off. And most important, don't panic and don't get upset. It's easy to get lost even in a small forest if the vegetation is thick and there are hills that distort your frame of reference. However, by using common sense and remembering a few landmarks, you'll easily find your way back.

Wildlife

As you ride, keep your eyes open for wildlife. Many animals, such as deer and turkey, won't immediately recognize a mountain biker, and sometimes you can ride right up and say hello. Squirrels and chipmunks are common, and if you are lucky, you might spot a pheasant or a fox. In the springtime, you can often hear, and sometimes see, the mighty pileated woodpecker hammering away at a tree. When riding along power line cuts, keep a look out for red tailed hawks and look for broad winged hawks when heading back into the woods. You might also see Peregrine falcons during migration. Look around while riding and you'll be amazed at what you find.

Dogs

The best way to ward off an attacking dog is to keep pedaling and shout "No!" or "Go home!" in an authoritative voice. "Get off the couch!" seems to be effective as well. If this doesn't work, just remember that it's not easy for a dog to bite when your legs are spinning, especially in a low gear. Don't be intimidated. Most dogs are territorial and will stop chasing after a short distance anyway.

After Your Ride

In order to keep a bike in top working order, keep it clean. One caveat: Use light pressure with your hose so water doesn't find it's way into your bicycle's bearings, where it can do more harm then good. Make sure to clean all the muck out of all chain rings. Then dry the bike off and lubricate the chain and any cables that are visible. After lubricating the chain, be sure to wipe it off with a rag to minimize the amount of dirt-attracting oil on the outside of the chain. Then wash the water bottles and all your cycling clothes so they don't stink up your house. Finally, grab some food, preferably something high-carb and low-fat. Such prompt refueling will help get you into better shape faster by nourishing your system when you need it most.

Westchester slickrock at Sprain Ridge Park.

RIDES IN
NEW YORK CITY, NEW YORK

1. CUNNINGHAM PARK

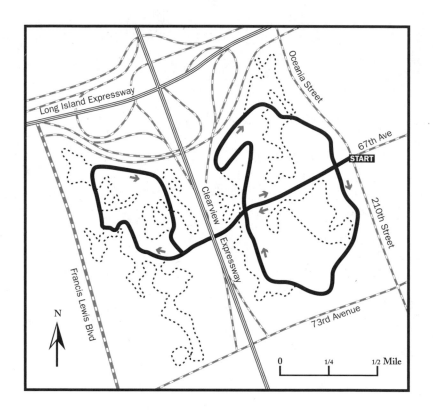

LOCATION:	Queens, New York
DISTANCE FROM NYC:	30 minutes (14 miles)
TRAILS DESCRIBED:	North Woods Trail
DIFFICULTY LEVEL:	Beginner

Overview

North Woods is one of only two official mountain-biking destinations within the five boroughs of New York City. North Woods, in Queens, opened in 2007 and riding is only allowed in the North Woods section of Cunningham Park, with 6 miles of one-way trails, effectively bisected by the Clearview Expressway. A fire road over a pedestrian bridge connects the two halves. There are no steep hills and very little elevation change, with predominantly fire roads and double track on the east side of the expressway and singletrack on the western side, all appropriately marked according to difficulty.

Directions by Car

From the East Side: Take the midtown tunnel (entrance on 2nd Avenue between 36th and 37th streets) out of Manhattan, traveling East on Interstate 495. Stay on 495 for approximately 12 miles until exit 27. Take the Clearview Expressway south for 1 mile and exit at 73rd Avenue. Turn left, go ¼ mile to 210th Street and turn left, trailhead is ¼ mile ahead at the corner of 67th Avenue.

Directions by Train

Take the F train to the last stop (179th Street & Hillside Avenue). Exit the front of the train and continue east on Hillside Avenue and turn left onto Midland Parkway. At the end, turn left onto 188th Street. At the next major intersection, turn right onto Union Turnpike. Then turn left at Francis Lewis Boulevard, right at 73rd Avenue, and left onto to 210th Street. The trailhead is at the corner of 210th and 67th avenues.

2. HIGHBRIDGE PARK

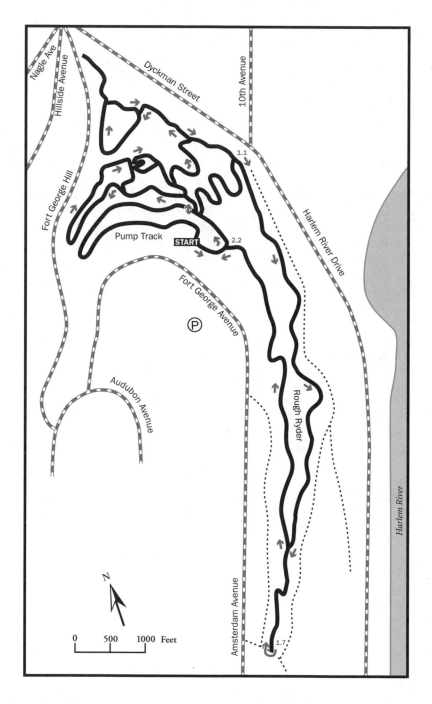

| LOCATION: | New York City, New York |
| TRAILS DESCRIBED: | Rough Ryder Loop |

Overview

Highbridge Park opened in May 2007 as the first and only official mountain bike park in Manhattan. Located near the northern tip of the island in Harlem, the trails are meticulously carved into a narrow hillside park located in a strip of land squeezed between the Amsterdam Avenue and Harlem River Drive. Despite its relatively small size, there is a dense mix of beginner, intermediate and advanced terrain along the 3 miles of trails, including a free-ride descent clearly marked with a double diamond and warning sign at the top. Given the long-standing ban on trail-riding in Central Park, we commend local officials for working with IMBA and local advocates to sanction and prepare an alternative for city-dwelling mountain-biking enthusiasts.

While many have waited years in anticipation and now finally have an official off-road destination in Manhattan, the park does have some drawbacks even beyond its small size. First, it is located a significant distance from most residents, such that if you choose to ride to the park, on-road time will likely be longer than off-road time. In addition, it is not the typical rural mountain-bike park experience: Many of the trails are littered with shards of broken glass, rats are the most abundant form of wildlife you'll see, and it is probably best not to ride here alone at any time. Finally, while the interior section of the park is heavily wooded, unfortunately there is significant growth of poison ivy bordering nearly every trail. One of the attractive additional features is the dirt jump park and pump track, located at the entrance to the trails, which includes both beginner and intermediate lines, with jumps, tables, and berms.

Directions by Car

From the East Side: Take Harlem River Drive north until it ends at the intersection of 10th Avenue. Turn left onto Dyckman Street. At the next intersection, turn left onto Fort George Hill and park on the left; the northern entrance to the park is on the left immediately before the guardrail. Alternatively, continue to drive up Fort George Hill. At the light at the top, make a sharp left turn onto Fort George Avenue which circles around and leads to much more parking, though the spaces can fill quickly if there are league games occurring. Here you will see the Fort George Playground on the left side, adjacent to the dirt jump park. The main trailhead is between the dirt jump park and the basketball court.

From the West Side: Take Amsterdam Avenue north until it ends at 190th Street and becomes Fort George Avenue. Continue about 3 more blocks and park near the baseball field on the right. The main trailhead is between the pump track and the basketball court (adjacent to the baseball field).

Directions by Train (subway)

Take the #1 train to Dyckman Street. At the intersection underneath the subway tracks, turn right onto Fort George Hill. The northern entrance to the park is on the left immediately before the guardrail. Alternatively, continue to ride up Fort George Hill. At the light at the top, make a sharp left turn onto Fort George Avenue which circles around and leads to the main park entrance. Here you will see the Fort George Playground on the left side, adjacent to the dirt jump park. The main trailhead is between the dirt jump park and the basketball court.

ڶڶ ROUGH RYDER LOOP

Trip Length:	2.20 miles
Difficulty:	Intermediate
Trail Configuration:	Loop
Elevation Change:	50 feet
Trail Type:	Singletrack

Pt. to Point	Cume	Turn	Landmark
0.00	0.00	**S**	Enter the park between the jump track on the left and the basketball court on the right.
0.10	0.10	**BR/BL**	You'll immediately come to a fork. Bear RIGHT and then continue to bear LEFT as you go around this fast beginner loop called "speedway."

Pt. to Point	Cume	Turn	Landmark
0.30	0.40	**BL**	When you see the jump track on the right, bear LEFT to a four-way intersection with two ways down. Unless you have your free-ride bike, take the more gradual descent to the left.
0.10	0.50	**BL**	Continue to bear LEFT, through an open area that takes you to the "wonderwall" drop-off or choose a jug handle escape.
0.20	0.70	**BR/L**	Bear RIGHT through the engine block section and then downhill and LEFT to circle around the skills loop.
0.20	0.90	**BL**	From the skills loop, bear LEFT and downhill as the trail becomes technical and muddy as it continues down toward street level near Dyckman and 10th Avenue.
0.20	1.10	**S**	You will see the bottom of the steep, free-ride Hellfire Trail on the right. Continue on the Rough Ryder trail to the southern boundary of the park.
0.60	1.70	**T/X**	Here the trail ends at an abandoned road with access to 190th Street and Amsterdam Avenue up to the right. Alternatively, to the left, the road parallels Amsterdam Avenue for another half mile, at a slightly lower elevation, and offers some good views of the Harlem River until it ends with steps down to the underpass beneath the Cross Bronx Expressway. At this point you can backtrack and then re-enter the park to continue north on Rough Ryder.
0.30	2.00	**S**	This trail is tight and technical. Unfortunately, there is also considerable growth of poison ivy along the sides of the trail.
0.20	2.20	**L**	After passing the baseball field on the left, turn LEFT at the next intersection to exit the park or right to head back for another loop.

RIDES IN
WESTCHESTER COUNTY, NEW YORK

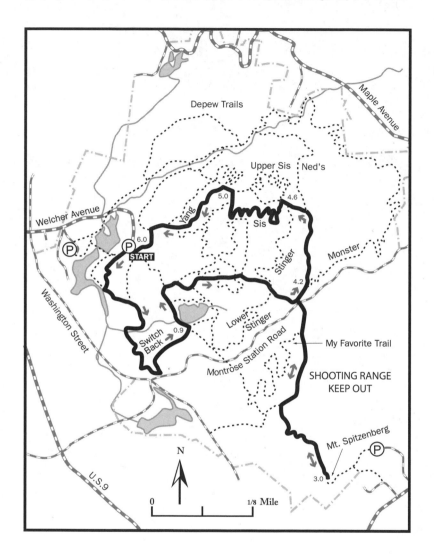

LOCATION:	Peekskill, New York
DISTANCE FROM NYC:	1 hour (44 miles)
TRAILS DESCRIBED:	Mt. Spitzenberg;
	Blue Mountain Carriage Trail

Overview

The Blue Mountain Reservation is a 1,600-acre multi-use park with dedicated, marked trails for mountain biking. The trail system consists of a system of wide, rocky carriage trail loops. Interconnecting these trails are numerous tight, technical singletrack trails that are detailed on the accompanying map. One relatively new trail is the Monster trail which goes along the northeast perimeter of the park. Unlike the other trails, it rarely intersects any other trail, so once you take this trail, you are committed to it!

The park is known for its magnificent rock formations of Hudson Highland granite and natural rock gardens. Blue Mountain is a popular destination for mountain bikers in Westchester County due to its varied terrain and steep climbs and descents. Once you ride here, you'll keep coming back. The two routes described below highlight the two predominant trail types at Blue Mountain: carriage trail and singletrack. The singletrack route contains some of the hillier and more technical sections of the carriage trail route. Both are challenging rides. There are a number of new singletrack sections that have been added to the trail system in the past few years. One of the best are the two trails known as Upper SIS and Lower SIS. SIS is an acronym for "snakes in space" and aptly describes the trails, which are both tight, twisting, and flowing singletrack near the top of the mountain. Apparently additional trails are in the works, especially throughout Depew Park, which is adjacent to Blue Mountain's northern border.

Directions by Car

From the West Side (57th Street): Take the West Side Highway (9A) north, which becomes the Henry Hudson Parkway. After approximately 8 miles, cross the Henry Hudson Bridge. Three miles later, the highway becomes the Saw Mill River Parkway. Continue for 2 more miles and exit at the Cross Country Parkway East. Take the Cross Country for approximately

2 miles and exit onto the Sprain Brook Parkway North, which will become the Taconic Parkway. Stay on the Sprain/Taconic for approximately 15 miles until the 9A/100 Exit (Don't take the earlier exit for 9A in Hawthorne). Stay on 9A for 6 additional miles, when 9A will merge with 9 North (follow the sign for Peekskill). Proceed on 9 North for 7 miles and exit at Welcher Avenue. At the light, turn right onto Welcher Avenue. The park is straight ahead, less than 1 mile. Enter the park, turn left at the stop sign near the guard station, and follow the road until it ends at a parking lot (about half of a mile).

From the East Side: Take the FDR (62nd Street entrance used for mileage calculations) for 3 miles to the Willis Avenue Bridge (Exit 18). Cross the bridge and follow the signs for 87 North (Deegan Expressway). Stay on 87 for 10 miles and exit at the Cross County Parkway East. Stay on the Cross County for 1 mile and exit onto the Sprain Brook Parkway North.

Directions by Train

Take the Metro North Hudson Line to Peekskill. Turn right upon exiting the train, then left up the hill on Requa Street. Turn right onto Washington Street at the stop sign. After 1 mile, turn left onto Welcher Avenue. Enter the park. Turn left at the guard station and follow the road until it ends at a parking lot.

武 *MT. SPITZENBERG*

Trip Length:	7.40 miles
Difficulty:	Advanced
Trail Configuration:	Loop with Out and Back
Elevation Change:	450 feet
Trail Type:	Singletrack, Carriage Trail

Pt. to Point	Cume	Turn	Landmark
0.00	0.00	S	Enter the trail just beyond the bike sign at the back of the parking lot.
0.10	0.10	**T/L**	Trail comes to a T-intersection. Turn LEFT.
0.10	0.20	**BR**	Main trail becomes a steep uphill. Bear RIGHT onto singletrack near a large rock,

Pt. to Point	Cume	Turn	Landmark
			following the orange blazes.
0.20	0.40	S	Cross over a stream.
0.10	0.50	L	Come to a grassy gas-line right-of-way. Turn LEFT. Follow the red blazes.
0.20	0.70	L	After a rock formation on the left and the main trail forks slightly off to the right, make a left onto singletrack on the left. (As a landmark, note a single trail dumping into the grassy section from the right. Also, make the LEFT turn before the trail becomes a steep climb.)
0.20	0.90	T/L/S	Trail ends at a T-intersection with a "not a horse trail" sign on a tree on the right side. Notice a pond straight ahead. (marker 13) Turn LEFT, following the orange blazes. After making this turn, note a trail to the right, then go over a stream bed, then note an opening for the pond on the right, then pass a trail on the right with a red marker on a tree. Continue STRAIGHT through all this.
0.20	1.10	R	Make a RIGHT when main trail forks (marker 5), following the orange/green blazes. Get ready for a twisty, challenging uphill climb.
0.20	1.30	BR	Stay RIGHT at the fork.
0.30	1.60	T/R	At the T-intersection, turn RIGHT, continuing with the orange/green blazes.
0.30	1.90	BL	The trail leads out of the woods and into grassy area. There will be a road off to the right and a trail merging from the right. Bear LEFT, staying on the main trail.
0.10	2.00	BR	Trail will fork. Stay RIGHT, travel down a short slope and across a dirt road (Montrose Station Road), onto the green/orange blazed trail on the other side (marker 25).
0.20	2.20	S	The trail is very rocky, with a slight uphill grade to it. To the right at a sharp angle is the

Pt. to Point	Cume	Turn	Landmark
			entrance to My Favorite Trail, a singletrack, more technical route that runs parallel for about a mile.
0.20	2.40	S	Enjoy a short, gradual descent.
0.10	2.50	L	Turn LEFT at the fork and continue uphill.
0.10	2.60	S	The climbing becomes strenuous as the grad of the trail steepens.
0.30	2.90	S	At the top of the hill, continue across an intersecting trail and walk your bike up the steep incline straight ahead.
0.10	3.00	S	Proceed past an abandoned house foundation and walk straight ahead to a few boulders perched just tight to afford a spectacular, panoramic view of the Southern Hudson Valley from the top of Mt. Spitzenberg.
0.10	3.10	X	Retrace the same route back to Montrose Station Road (mile 2.00). The ride back will be exceedingly fast and bumpy.
1.10	4.20	R/L	Proceed back across the road, turn RIGHT onto the gas line right of way, then quickly turn LEFT and head back into the woods.
0.10	4.30	BL	Bear LEFT at the fork, following the circular orange and green blazes (marker 29). (*Note*: the trail to the right leads to the MYX Monster trail, a long singletrack that travels along the northeast perimeter of the park.)
0.20	4.50	S	Notice a trail merging in from the right. Stay STRAIGHT.
0.10	4.60	S	Stay STRAIGHT. [Alternate route for a challenging singletrack descent to the parking lot: proceed left at marker 31 and then turn onto the second singletrack (Upper SIS). At the next intersection, turn right onto crossover, then a left at marker 44 onto Yang which ends at marker 41. Turn left and then head to the parking lot.]
0.50	5.10	L	At the bottom of a descent, trail will fork. Stay LEFT (marker 32).

Pt. to Point	Cume	Turn	Landmark
0.20	5.30	R/R	Cross over a bridge over a stream bed and at the top of an incline make a RIGHT onto a singletrack trail (marker 35). Make a RIGHT at the next fork. Follow the blue and orange "V" blazes.
0.20	5.50	BL	Stay LEFT at fork.
0.10	5.60	S	Cross over a small stream.
0.10	5.70	L/L	Trail ends at a paved road. Make LEFT onto road, then make immediate LEFT back onto singletrack trail.
0.10	5.80	L	Turn LEFT at the fork. Go up and around some fallen trees and be careful on the ensuing descent.
0.10	5.90	S	A trail goes off to the right. Continue STRAIGHT.
0.20	6.10	BL/L	Trail will descend and bear to the LEFT at the clearing with horse shoe pits on the right. Turn LEFT and continue along trail with lake to the right.
0.10	6.20	L/BR	At the end of the lake there is a red shack. Turn LEFT onto a small trail. Bear RIGHT at the next fork, which leads to a carriage road.
0.10	6.30	L	Make a LEFT at the carriage road, which leads up a short hill and past two old sheds, then down a hill and over a bridge to another intersection.
0.20	6.50	L	Make a LEFT at the intersection and then continue down the hill, over another bridge.
0.20	6.70	S	The singletrack will empty onto a gravely carriage trail. Continue STRAIGHT.
0.30	7.00	L	Trail ends at road. Turn LEFT.
0.40	7.40	S	You are back at your car.

ᚶ BLUE MOUNTAIN CARRIAGE TRAIL

Trip Length:	3.60 miles	
Difficulty:	Intermediate	
Trail Configuration:	Loop	
Elevation Change:	320 feet	
Trail Type:	Carriage Trail	

Pt. to Point	Cume	Turn	Landmark
0.00	0.00	S	Go back to the front of the parking lot and enter the park near the signs. Be sure to warm up first because the trail begins with a rocky steep uphill climb.
0.10	0.10	S	Continue STRAIGHT, notice a footpath on the left, then a trail to the right. Be prepared for more climbing.
0.10	0.20	S	Trail winds left and continues uphill.
0.10	0.30	L	Turn LEFT onto main trail. Get ready for a twisty, challenging uphill climb.
0.20	0.50	R	Stay RIGHT at the fork.
0.30	0.80	T/R	At the T-intersection, turn RIGHT.
0.30	1.10	BL	The trail leads out of the woods and into a grassy area. There will be a road off to the right and a trail merging from the right. Bear LEFT, staying on the main trail.
0.10	1.20	L	Trail will fork. Stay LEFT here and head back into the woods.
0.10	1.30	BL	Bear LEFT at the fork.
0.20	1.50	S	Notice a trail merging in from the right. Stay STRAIGHT.
0.10	1.60	S	Notice a footpath on the left. Stay STRAIGHT.
0.50	2.10	BL	At the bottom of a descent, trail will fork. Stay LEFT.
0.20	2.30	BL	Cross over a bridge over a stream bed and at the top of an incline, stay LEFT (notice a singletrack trail on the right).
0.10	2.40	S	Stay STRAIGHT as the trail gradually

Pt. to Point	Cume	Turn	Landmark
			descends. Notice a footpath and a creek on the left.
0.20	2.60	S	Stay STRAIGHT as the trail flattens out. Notice another footpath on the left.
0.30	2.90	L	As the trail continues downhill, follow the main trail to the LEFT.
0.30	3.20	L	Trail ends at road. Turn LEFT.
0.40	3.60	S	You are back at your car.

Boulder hopping in Blue Mountain.

4. BRONX RIVER PATHWAY

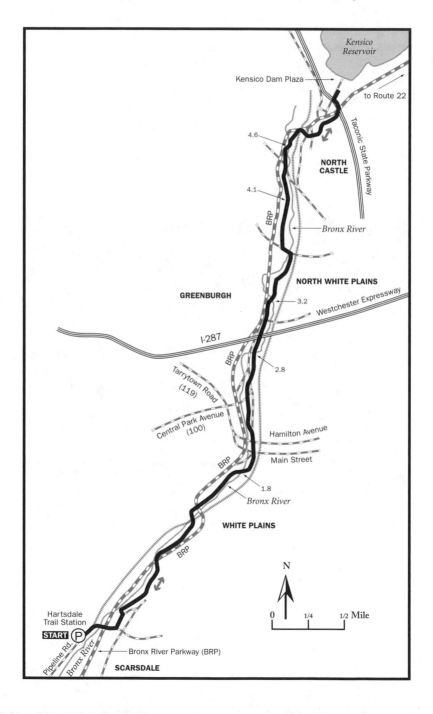

LOCATION:	Hartsdale, New York
DISTANCE FROM NYC:	45 minutes (22 miles)
TRAILS DESCRIBED:	Bronx River Pathway,
	Kensico Dam Plaza

Overview

The Bronx River Pathway is part of the Bronx River Reservation, an 807-acre linear park that was built at the same time as the Bronx River Parkway, between 1907 and 1925. During that time, workers planted 30,000 trees and 140,000 shrubs along the parkway and the river. The Bronx River Pathway is a narrow, gently rolling trailway, 80 percent of which is asphalt pavement. The rest is a dirt trail. The Bronx River Parkway was the first highway to be built in the United States. The pathway ends in Valhalla at the 30 billion gallon Kensico Reservoir, which supplies water to nearly nine million people in New York City and Westchester County. By the way, don't expect to see a roaring river near the pathway. The Bronx "River" is more like a stream or creek than a bona fide river.

Directions by Car

From the West Side (57th Street): Take the West Side Highway (9A) north, which becomes the Henry Hudson Parkway. After approximately 8 miles cross the Henry Hudson Bridge. Three miles later, the highway becomes the Saw Mill River Parkway. Continue for 2 more miles and exit at the Cross County Parkway East. Take the Cross County for approximately 2 miles and exit onto the Bronx River Parkway North and continue for 7 miles to Exit 15 (Fenimore Road/Hartsdale). At the exit, turn left, cross over the Parkway, then make the first right into the Hartsdale train station parking lot and park there.

From the East Side: Take the FDR (62nd Street entrance used for mileage calculations) for 3 miles to the Willis Avenue Bridge (Exit 18). Cross the bridge and follow the signs for 87 North (Deegan Expressway).

Stay on 87 for 10 miles and exit at the Cross County Parkway East Stay on the Cross County for 1 mile and exit onto the Bronx River Parkway North and continue for 7 miles to Exit 15 (Fenimore Road/Hartsdale). At the exit, turn left, cross over the Parkway, then make the first right into the Hartsdale train station parking lot and park there.

Note: Drivers living closer to the northern end of the trail near Valhalla may want to start at Kensico Dam Plaza and follow these directions in reverse.

Directions by Train

Take Metro North Harlem Line to Hartsdale.

᧒ᚖ BRONX RIVER PATHWAY, KENSICO DAM PLAZA

Trip Length:	10.40 miles
Difficulty:	Beginner
Trail Configuration:	Out and Back
Elevation Change:	50 feet
Trail Type:	Pavement

Pt. to Point	Cume	Turn	Landmark
0.00	0.00	L	From the bottom of the stairs at the Hartsdale Train Station parking lot, ride LEFT out of the lot and onto the bridge over the Bronx River Parkway. Note a church in front of you.
0.10	0.10	L/L	At the stop sign, make a LEFT onto the trail. Notice a blue sign for the trail. Once on the trail, stay LEFT at the fork.
0.10	0.20	S	Travel past the pond on the right and a tennis club on the left. The river and the parkway are on your left; a steep slope with houses on top is on the right.
0.40	0.60	S	The trail goes up a slight grade.
0.10	0.70	S	Go over a small wooden bridge.
0.10	0.80	S	The trail winds down and to the left. Watch your head as you go under a very low bridge. There are train tracks on the other side of the river.
0.20	1.00	S	Go down a short downhill.
0.20	1.20	S	Cross over a wooden bridge. The trail is paved from this point forward.
0.10	1.30	S	Cross under the railroad, then over the river on a bridge, and then under a large highway bridge.

Pt. to Point	Cume	Turn	Landmark
0.50	1.80	R	Cross back over the river on a bridge, go up a slight hill, and stay RIGHT at the fork.
0.20	2.00	S	The trail comes to an intersection at a main road in White Plains. Wait with the traffic for the light and be careful as you continue STRAIGHT across the two main roads.
0.20	2.20	L	Make a LEFT when there is a pedestrian tunnel to the White Plains train station on the right.
0.20	2.40	S	Enter the parking lot with the Westchester County Center on the left. Go STRAIGHT across to where the trail picks up on the other side.
0.20	2.60	S	Cross over a road.
0.20	2.80	S	Cross over the river on a bridge.
0.10	2.90	S	Cross under Interstate 287.
0.20	3.10	S	Cross over a road.
0.10	3.20	S	Cross back over the river on a bridge.
0.30	3.50	L/L	The trail comes to a road with a pedestrian tunnel straight ahead. Make a LEFT, go through a parking lot, and turn LEFT again onto the road, which crosses over a metal bridge.
0.20	3.70	R	After the bridge, make a RIGHT back onto the path.
0.40	4.10	S	Cross over another road.
0.30	4.40	S	Cross over another road.
0.20	4.60	S	Cross over a bridge, then up a slight grade.
0.20	4.80	S	Cross over the Bronx River Parkway Memorial Bridge over the Harlem Line train tracks.
0.10	4.90	S	Cross over a road. There is a ball field on the right.
0.20	5.10	S	Go under a bridge.
0.10	5.20	R	Cross over the road and enter Kensico Dam Plaza. The dam is straight ahead. If you feel like doing some climbing, take a RIGHT and go up the red brick road to the top of the dam. It's about a half mile to the top of the bridge over the dam. There is a great view of the reservoir on the right and the Plaza down below on the left.

5. GRAHAM HILLS PARK

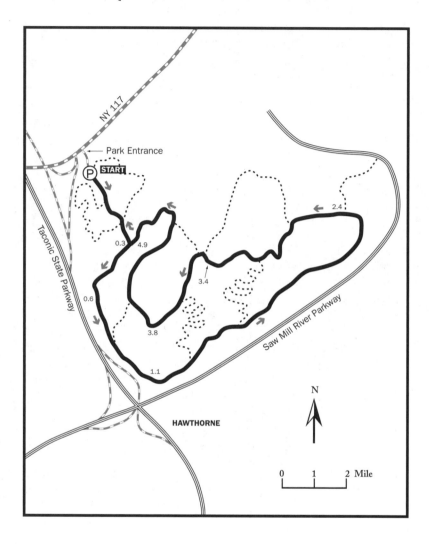

NY 117

Park Entrance

P START

Taconic State Parkway

0.3 4.9

2.4

3.4

0.6

3.8

Saw Mill River Parkway

1.1

HAWTHORNE

N

0   1   2 Mile

LOCATION:	Pleasantville, New York
DISTANCE FROM NYC:	45 minutes (27 miles)
TRAILS DESCRIBED:	Graham Hills MTB Trail

Overview

Graham Hills Park is a dedicated mountain-biking park located in the middle of Westchester County, at the junction of the Taconic and Saw Mill River parkways. The immaculately groomed trails offer a rollicking roller coaster of a ride. Make sure you are in good shape before venturing to Graham Hills, because the trails toward the middle of the park are quite steep, with two sections offering vertical climbs of over 300 feet through a distance of only 0.5 miles. The 431-acre park has a total of 8 miles of trails through three sets of loops. The park is thickly wooded. After the swampy part at the entrance, there are only a few water crossings on the outside loop, but a few creeks cascade down the southern side of the park. The maximum elevation is 611 feet, and while the trails pass over the peak, don't expect much of a view, because the top is heavily wooded. The Park is named for Dr. Isaac Gilbert Graham, a Revolutionary War surgeon who settled there in 1785.

Directions by Car

From the West Side (57th Street): Take the West Side Highway (9A) north, which becomes the Henry Hudson Parkway. After approximately 8 miles cross the Henry Hudson Bridge. Three miles later, the highway becomes the Saw Mill River Parkway. Continue for 2 more miles and exit at the Cross County Parkway East. Take the Cross County for approximately 2 miles and exit onto the Sprain Brook Parkway North, which will become the Taconic Parkway. Continue on the Sprain/Taconic for about 14 miles to the Pleasantville Road Exit. Turn right and make the next immediate right into the park.

From the East Side: Take the FDR (62nd Street entrance used for mileage calculations) for 3 miles to the Willis Avenue Bridge (Exit 18). Cross the bridge and follow the signs for 87 North (Deegan Expressway).

Stay on 87 for 10 miles and exit at the Cross County Parkway East. Stay on the Cross County for 1 mile and exit onto the Sprain Brook Parkway North. Continue with West Side Directions.

Directions by Train

Take the Metro North Harlem Line to Pleasantville. Exit the southern side of the train and proceed up the stairs. Turn right onto Bedford Road. At 0.2 miles, turn left at the light above the Saw Mill River Parkway, following the signs for 117. Travel 0.3 miles and at the stop sign, turn right continuing on 117 (Bedford Road). Continue 0.5 miles; shortly after passing Pace University on the right, turn left into Graham Hills Park.

ൟ GRAHAM HILL MTB TRAIL

Trip Length:	5.20 miles
Difficulty:	Intermediate/Advanced
Trail Configuration:	Loop
Elevation Change:	350 feet
Trail Type:	Singletrack

Pt. to Point	Cume	Turn	Landmark
0.00	0.00	BL	Enter the park at the trail at the back of the parking lot. Follow the yellow/blue trail down a slight grade and through a section of mud and rocks and two bridges over particularly gooey areas. Bear LEFT at the first fork.
0.30	0.30	R	Make a RIGHT turn at the fork onto the blue-blazed trail.
0.30	0.60	S	After a very fast descent, with ample bumps perfect for refining (or developing) jumping technique, the trail flattens out along a grassy area before heading back into the woods.
0.30	0.90	S	Ride alongside a fence that separates the park from the Taconic Parkway in the

Pt. to Point	Cume	Turn	Landmark
			distance. (The fence is a nice safety measure that prevents errant deer, and cyclists, from wandering onto the Parkway.) Stay in a relatively low gear to be able to climb the many short, steep rises that this section of the park supplies.
0.20	1.10	S	Cross over a stone fence, which marks the southern tip of this diamond-shaped park. The merging Taconic and Saw Mill parkways are visible in the distance.
0.10	1.20	S	Ride through a rock garden as the trail turns north.
0.20	1.40	S	The trail continues to be interesting, with some sharp turns, quick roller-coaster climbs and descents, with a few stream crossings to dampen your feet. Steep cliffs become visible on the left, and the Saw Mill River (which is more like a small stream) on the right.
0.30	1.70	BR	Stay RIGHT at the fork. The green-blazed and orange-blazed trails on the left are challenging short cuts leading to higher elevations in the park.
0.20	1.90	S	Pass two stone house foundations.
0.20	2.10	S	The trail flattens out for a stretch— conserve your energy because the real climbing begins soon. Pass trail to the left.
0.30	2.40	S	Continue STRAIGHT past an interesting trail (leads to Saw Mill River Parkway, Thornwood Exit) on the right.
0.20	2.60	BL	Bear to the LEFT as you enter a former motocross training area. There are multiple trails here; keep to the singletrack on the far left. The red-blazed trail on the right is an alternate route up to reach the park summit.
0.10	2.70	R	Follow blue blazes to the right at fork.
0.10	2.80	BL	Continue to stay LEFT as you approach a three-way fork. The elevation here is about

Pt. to Point	Cume	Turn	Landmark
			325 feet. The next 0.5 miles cover 250 feet in elevation, so gear down and get ready for a tough climb. This part of the trail was recently converted from breakneck climb to a series of challenging switchbacks.
0.30	3.10	**BR**	Stay RIGHT at fork, continuing the ascent.
0.20	3.30	**S**	Take a break at a landing to enjoy the view (Graham Hills is tree-covered, even at its peak, so the view is visible only in winter). You are not yet at the top.
0.10	3.40	**L**	Reach the top of the hill (611 feet), pass a trail on the right and turn LEFT at the next fork onto the white-blazed trail.
0.10	3.50	**S**	Enjoy a fast, steep, narrow descent.
0.20	3.70	**S**	The trail traverses two stone walls.
0.10	3.80	**S**	The trail flattens out and winds around to the right.
0.20	4.00	**R**	Turn RIGHT at the fork, following the white blazes.
0.30	4.30	**BL**	Bear LEFT as the trail ascends to the top of a hill.
0.20	4.50	**L**	Turn LEFT onto the blue/yellow trail. Notice a few houses on the right. The trail gradually descends, turns sharply to the left and levels off. (Alternative route: Stay straight instead of left and enjoy a concentrated back and forth singletrack ride, which reconnects to the trail you were on.)
0.40	4.90	**BR**	Stay RIGHT at the fork at the intersection with the blue trail from mile 0.3.
0.20	5.10	**S**	Cross over two bridges and through the muddy section from the beginning of the ride.
0.10	5.20	**S**	Return to the parking lot.

Log crossing in Graham Hills.

Photo by Jennifer Sendek

6. NORTH COUNTY TRAILWAY

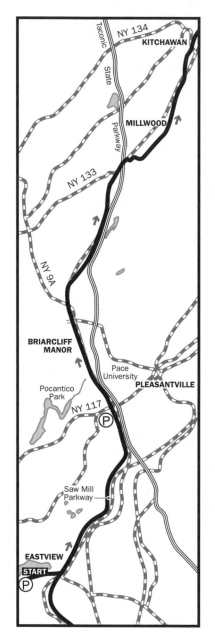

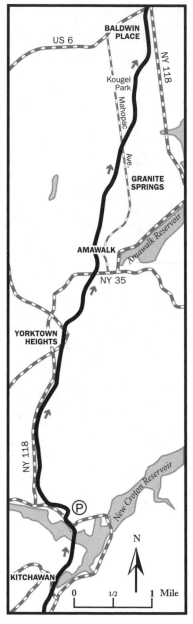

NY 134
Taconic
State
Parkway
KITCHAWAN
MILLWOOD
NY 133
NY 9A
BRIARCLIFF MANOR
Pace University
Pocantico Park
NY 117
Ⓟ
PLEASANTVILLE
Saw Mill Parkway
EASTVIEW
START
Ⓟ

US 6
BALDWIN PLACE
NY 118
Kougel Park
Mahopac Ave.
GRANITE SPRINGS
Amawalk Reservoir
AMAWALK
NY 35
YORKTOWN HEIGHTS
NY 118
Ⓟ
New Croton Reservoir
KITCHAWAN
N
0   1/2   1 Mile

LOCATION:	Tarrytown, New York
DISTANCE FROM NYC:	45 minutes (25 miles)
TRAILS DESCRIBED:	Eastview Trail

Overview

The North County Trailway is constructed on land that was formerly the right-of-way for the Putnam Division of the New York Central Railroad. This railroad provided commuter rail service between the Bronx and Brewster from 1881 to 1958. Nationwide, many of the 2,000 miles of track that are abandoned each year are converted to trailways through the rails-to-trails program. This program began as a result of the National Trails Systems Act (1983). Since these are former railroad beds (the ties have been removed), they are virtually flat. Railroad beds were designed to rise no more than two degrees from level. The North County Trailway is not only flat, but is has also been paved for recreational use. As a result, it is a good destination for those who are new to mountain biking and want to build up confidence before plunging into true "off-road" riding. This is good preparation for riding on carriage roads and singletrack, which can be intimidating to beginners. This type of trail is also a great destination for families with small children. While this trailway is paved, it is still quite remote and cuts through a thick forest and some stunning rock formations. (The first 1.3 miles of the trailway, from Tarrytown to the old Eastview train station, were not part of the old Putnam Line.)

Directions by Car

From the West Side (57th Street): Take the West Side Highway (9A) north, which becomes the Henry Hudson Parkway. After approximately 8 miles cross the Henry Hudson Bridge. Three miles later, the highway becomes the Saw Mill River Parkway. Continue for 13 more miles until Exit 23 (Eastview). At the light, turn left, go through the next light, and proceed 1.5 miles around the lakes to a parking lot on the right. Sunnyside Avenue will be on the left. Park in the lot.

From the East Side: Take the FDR (62nd Street entrance used for mileage calculations) for 3 miles to the Willis Avenue Bridge (Exit 18). Cross the bridge and follow the signs for 87 North (Deegan Expressway).

Stay on 87 for 7 miles and exit at the Saw Mill River Parkway North. Stay on the Saw Mill for 13 additional miles until Exit 23 (Eastview). Continue with West Side Directions.

Directions by Train

Note: The trip from the train station to the trailhead is mostly uphill! Take the Metro North Hudson Division Line to Tarrytown. Depart the train, and ride around to the right of the parking lot. Go straight at the first stop sign and bear left at the next stop sign, ahead toward White Street. This is a short, steep road which bears right onto Main Street in Tarrytown. At 0.5 miles, cross over Route 9 (South Broadway) and proceed up the steep Neperan Road, which winds left then right and passes through Fordham University. Approximately 1 mile from the train station, when there is a parking lot on the left, turn right onto Sunnyside Avenue. The trailhead is on the left side of Sunnyside Avenue.

*Alternative for northern section of North County Trailway (see map):*Take the Metro North Harlem Line to Pleasantville. Exit the southern side of the train and proceed up the stairs. Turn right onto Bedford Road. At 0.2 miles, turn LEFT at the light above the Saw Mill River Parkway, following the signs for 117. Travel 0.3 miles and at the stop sign, turn right continuing on 117 (Bedford Road). Continue 0.8 miles; passing Pace University on the right, Graham Hills Park on the left. After passing Route 9A, the entrance to the northern section of the North County Trailway is on the right, and the entrance to the southern section is on the left.

۶ *EASTVIEW TRAIL*

Trip Length:	10.00 miles
Difficulty:	Beginner
Trail Configuration:	Out and Back
Elevation Change:	50 feet
Trail Type:	Pavement

Pt. to Point	Cume	Turn	Landmark
0.00	0.00	S	The trail begins across the street from the parking lot, near Sunnyside Avenue. Carefully cross the street and enter the trailway.

Pt. to Point	Cume	Turn	Landmark
0.30	0.30	S	Cross over an intersecting road.
0.60	0.90	S	The trail comes out of the woods and runs adjacent to Tarrytown Reservoir on the left.
0.10	1.00	S	Follow the trail downhill, to the right of the reservoir maintenance building.
0.10	1.10	R	The trail ends at Old Saw Mill River Road. Carefully cross the road and make a RIGHT onto the sidewalk on the other side of the road where the trail continues.
0.10	1.20	L	Follow the bicycle path sign to the LEFT and uphill.
0.10	1.30	T/BL	At the bottom of the hill, bear LEFT at the T-intersection. (A right leads to the southbound, portion of the trailway.) This is now the old Putnam Line right-of-way. Notice abandoned railroad tracks underneath the undergrowth on the left.
0.50	1.80	S	As the trail comes into a clearing, note the Saw Mill River and the Saw Mill River Parkway to the right.
0.40	2.20	S	The trail winds left. Pedaling along the flat trail, notice the steep hillside and high cliffs on the left.
0.40	2.60	S	The trail continues winding left and goes through another clearing with powerlines crossing overhead.
0.70	3.30	S	The trail straightens out. Notice more sheer cliffs and impressive rock outcroppings on the left.
0.20	3.50	S	Pass a dirt path on the right, which leads to a police station.
1.50	5.00	S	The trail passes under Route 117 and continues north. (*Note*: To access Graham Hills Park, exit at 117 and turn right. The entrance to Graham Hills will be on your right, approximately 1 mile east on Route 117.) *Turn around to complete the 10 mile out and back or continue up to 20 miles north until the trail ends at the Putnam County border.*

7. OLD CROTON AQUEDUCT

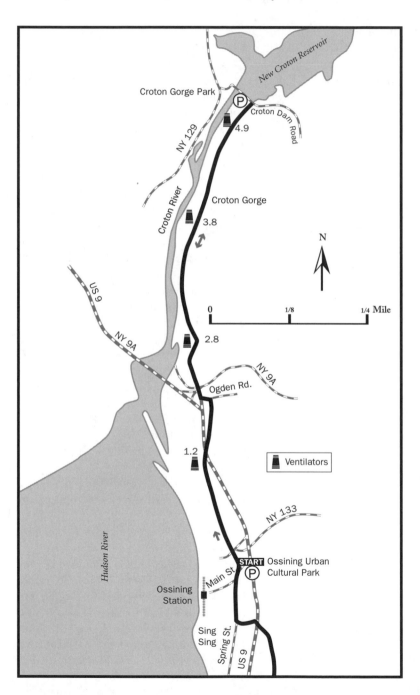

New Croton Reservoir

Croton Gorge Park

Croton Dam Road

4.9

NY 129

Croton River

Croton Gorge

3.8

N

US 9

NY 9A

0   1/8   1/4 Mile

2.8

NY 9A

Ogden Rd.

1.2

Ventilators

NY 133

Hudson River

START Ossining Urban
P   Cultural Park

Main St.

Ossining
Station

Sing
Sing

Spring St.

US 9

LOCATION:	Croton, New York
DISTANCE FROM NYC:	1 hour (40 miles)
TRAILS DESCRIBED:	Ossining-Croton Trail;
	Croton Trail

Overview

The Old Croton Aqueduct is an underground pipe that runs from the Croton Reservoir to Manhattan. The first of its kind ever constructed in the United States, the Aqueduct provided an integral link between the Croton watershed and the New York City population it served from 1842 until 1955. The trail above it is wide, smooth, and generally flat. Two overlapping sections of the Aqueduct Trail are described here. Train travelers should follow the Ossining-to-Croton trail description, while drivers should follow the Croton Trail description. There are a few steep hills in the Ossining-to-Croton section of the Aqueduct trail which make this ride more strenuous endeavor than just the Croton section. These hills are the result of highways and roads that were built over the Aqueduct and caused an interruption of the Aqueduct trail's right of way. There are no such interruptions of the Croton section of the Aqueduct trail.

Directions by Car (to Croton Trail)

From the West Side (57th Street): Take the West Side Highway (9A) north, which becomes the Henry Hudson Parkway. After approximately 8 miles cross the Henry Hudson Bridge. Three miles later, the highway becomes the Saw Mill River Parkway. Continue for 2 more miles and exit at the Cross County Parkway East. Take the Cross County for approximately 2 miles and exit onto the Sprain Brook Parkway North, which becomes the Taconic Parkway. Stay on the Sprain/Taconic for 15 miles until the 9A/100 Exit—Don't take the earlier exit for 9A in Hawthorne. Stay on 9A for 6 additional miles, when 9A will merge with 9 North (follow sign for Peekskill). Proceed on 9 North for 1 mile and take the 9A/129 Exit. Turn right at the stop sign and follow 129 for approximately 2 miles and turn right into Croton Gorge Park. Cross over the bridge and park in the lot at the base of the dam.

From the East Side: Take the FDR (62nd Street entrance used for mileage calculations) for 3 miles to the Willis Avenue Bridge (Exit 18). Cross the bridge and follow the signs for 87 North (Deegan Expressway).

Stay on 87 for 10 miles and exit at the Cross County Parkway East. Stay on the Cross County for 1 mile and exit onto the Sprain Brook Parkway North. Continue with West Side Directions.

Directions by Train (to Ossining-Croton Trail)

Take the Metro North Hudson Division Line to Ossining. Depart the train, and walk up the stairs to Secor Road, which crosses over the railroad tracks. Take this road away from the river (up the steep hill— this will get your heart rate going) until it flattens out and becomes Main Street in downtown Ossining. Go straight through the traffic light at approximately one half mile from the railroad station, and at the fork at the pedestrian crosswalk, stay left and ride onto the sidewalk. Notice the beginning of an urban pathway on the left in front of Parisi's Steakhouse. This is the Aqueduct trail and it is marked by pink bricks in the roadway and an "Old Croton Aqueduct" sign.

🚲 OSSINING-CROTON TRAIL

Trip Length:	10.60 miles
Difficulty:	Intermediate
Trail Configuration:	Out and Back
Elevation Change:	120 feet
Trail Type:	Carriage Trail

Pt. to Point	Cume	Turn	Landmark
0.00	0.00	S	Begin in Ossining on the brick trailway in front of Parisi's Steakhouse and between the retail shops on the left and right.
0.10	0.10	S	The path crosses over a bridge spanning the Sing Sing Kill, a steep gorge leading to the Hudson River.
0.10	0.20	L	Next is a weir station (a former holding station for the Aqueduct). Travel LEFT

Pt. to Point	Cume	Turn	Landmark
			around the station, across the road and up a set of stairs and down through a small playground.
0.10	0.30	S	Cross over the road.
0.10	0.40	S	Cross over another road.
0.10	0.50	S	Cross the road and stay to the right of the firehouse. The trail slowly transforms itself from a urban path to a rural trail. There are some houses on the right.
0.40	0.90	S	The trail seems to end at a grassy field. Keep going STRAIGHT, in front of an old stone house on the left. The trail continues on the other side of the field.
0.20	1.10	BR/BL	The trail stops at Route 9. Bear RIGHT off the trail, cross over Route 9, and bear LEFT onto the sidewalk and pick up the trail on the other side of the road following the signs.
0.30	1.40	S	After riding along a few backyards, the trail suddenly becomes very steep. Walk your bike up and cross the road. Be careful on the descent on the other side.
0.30	1.70	L	After going past some condominiums, turn LEFT onto the next road, down a hill. (The trail continues straight ahead but dead ends at a highway.)
0.10	1.80	R	At the bottom of the hill, turn RIGHT onto Albany Post Road. Go under bridge.
0.30	2.10	R/L	Turn RIGHT onto Shady Lane Farm Road and soon thereafter turn LEFT again onto a trail bordering a fence. There is a GE plant on the right.
0.30	2.40	S	Cross over Fowler; stay straight through. two large concrete slabs. The remainder of the ride is completely rural.
0.30	2.70	S	Cross over the road.
0.10	2.80	S	Notice a vent over the Aqueduct. There are a number of these 15-foot-high cylindrical cement structures.

Pt. to Point	Cume	Turn	Landmark
0.30	3.10	S	On the grassy landing, there is a fantastic view of the Hudson River in the distance. In the winter the Croton River is visible down below as it meanders its way to the Hudson.
0.20	3.30	S	Notice the very steep and impressive Croton Gorge on the left.
0.30	3.60	S	Cross over the road. At this point, the left side of the trail drops precipitously down to the Croton River, which you can hear rushing by down below.
0.20	3.80	S	Pass another vent.
0.30	4.10	S	Notice a stream running under the trail and a waterfall on the right side.
0.10	4.20	S	Cross over a road.
0.10	4.30	S	Pass through an impressive split rock formation.
0.50	4.80	S	Pass a few spur trails on the left and a steep trail on the right leading up to the power lines overhead.
0.10	4.90	S	Pass another vent.
0.20	5.10	S	Notice a sign, "Old Croton Trail Way State Park." Shortly thereafter, cross diagonally over a gravel road.
0.10	5.20	R/L	Next comes a landing where there is a nice view of the Croton Dam Park and the waterfall straight ahead and to the left. After the landing, turn RIGHT up a small hill, then LEFT at the top of the hill.
0.10	5.30	L/X	Trail ends at Croton Dam Road. Turn LEFT and head toward the bridge for a closer look at the waterfall. After that, turn around and head back.

🚲 CROTON TRAIL

Trip Length:	5.80 miles
Difficulty:	Beginner
Trail Configuration:	Out and Back
Elevation Change:	40 feet
Trail Type:	Carriage Trail

Pt. to Point	Cume	Turn	Landmark
0.00	0.00	S	Walk your bike into the Croton Gorge Park and up the hill, parallel to the dam. At the top is the start of the Aqueduct trail.
0.10	0.10	R	Turn RIGHT. The trail from this point on is consistently flat doubletrack.
0.10	0.20	S	Diagonally cross back over the gravel road. Notice a sign, "Old Croton Trail Way State Park."
0.20	0.40	S	Notice a vent over the Aqueduct. There are a number of these 15-foot-high cylindrical cement structures.
0.10	0.50	S	Pass a few spurs trails on the right and a steep trail on the left leading up to the power lines overhead.
0.50	1.00	S	Pass through an impressive split rock formation.
0.10	1.10	S	Cross over the road.
0.10	1.20	S	Notice a stream running under the trail and a waterfall on the left side.
0.30	1.50	S	Pass another vent.
0.20	1.70	S	Cross over the road. At this point, the right side of the trail drops precipitously down to the Croton River, which you can hear rushing by down below.
0.30	2.00	S	Notice the very steep and impressive Croton Gorge on the right.
0.20	2.20	S	On the grassy landing there is a fantastic view of the Hudson River in the distance. In the winter the Croton River down below

Pt. to Point	Cume	Turn	Landmark
			is visible as it meanders its way to the Hudson.
0.30	2.50	S	Pass another Aqueduct vent.
0.10	2.60	S	Cross over a road.
0.30	2.90	X	Trail ends at the road in front of the GE plant. At this point, it is possible to continue south to Ossining by following the Ossining section of this trail in reverse (at mile 2.4). Otherwise, turn back. The Croton section is much more scenic.

The Croton Trail is easy enough for the smallest mountain bikers.

8. SPRAIN RIDGE PARK

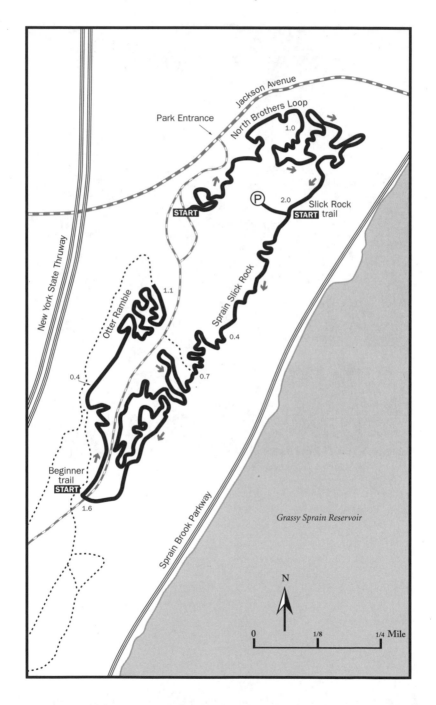

LOCATION:	Yonkers, New York
DISTANCE FROM NYC:	35 minutes (20 miles)
TRAILS DESCRIBED:	North Trail; Slick Rock trail;
	Otter Ramble

Overview

Sprain Ridge Park is a dedicated mountain-biking park in southern Westchester County. It is a narrow, rectangular park located in a 278-acre strip of land squeezed between the NYS Thruway on the west and the Sprain Brook Parkway on the east. Despite its relatively small size, the trails in the park are quite dense and appeal to both beginners and advanced riders. Beginners will find trails with limited obstacles and with limited climbing. Advanced riders will find other trails in the park that offer some of the most technical riding in Westchester with plentiful log crossings and rock gardens amid a switchback trail layout. Of particular interest to more advanced riders is the trails section set up amid a cleared area adjacent to the trail network.

To orient yourself, the park entrance is at the northern boundary of the park; park at the first (northern-most) parking lot. Two trailheads begin at opposite sides of this large parking area. A paved road runs south through the center of the park and leads to an unpaved doubletrack trail that continues until the southern border of the park.

Directions by Car

From the West Side (57th Street): Take the West Side Highway (9A) north, which becomes the Henry Hudson Parkway. After approximately 8 miles, cross the Henry Hudson Bridge. Three miles later, the highway becomes the Saw Mill River Parkway. Continue for 2 more miles and exit at the Cross Country Parkway East. Take the Cross Country for approximately 2 miles and exit onto the Sprain Brook Parkway North. Stay on the Sprain for approximately 3 miles until the Jackson Avenue Exit. Follow Jackson Avenue west for about a quarter mile, and the park entrance is on your left. Bear right as the entrance road becomes one-way and then bear left at the next fork and turn right into the first parking lot at the top of the hill.

From the East Side: Take the FDR (62nd Street entrance used for mileage calculations) for 3 miles to the Willlis Avenue Bridge (Exit 18). Cross the bridge and follow the signs for 87 North (Deegan Expressway). Stay on 87 for 10 miles and exit at the Cross County Parkway East. Stay on the Cross County for 1 mile and exit onto the Sprain Brook Parkway North. Continue with West Side directions.

Directions by Train

Take the Metro North Harlem line to the Tuckahoe Station and follow Tuckahoe Road West to East Grassy Sprain Road and make a right. Ride parallel to the highway approximately 2 to 3 miles and then turn left on Jackson Avenue. Go about a quarter mile, and the park entrance is on your left.

♾ NORTH TRAIL

Trip Length:	2.00 miles
Difficulty:	Intermediate
Trail Configuration:	One Way
Elevation Change:	150 feet
Trail Type:	Singletrack

Pt. to Point	Cume	Turn	Landmark
0.00	0.00	S	Enter in back near corner of the north parking lot (lot closest to the Jackson Avenue entrance), up a steep slope which then descends to a log-crossing.
0.20	0.20	S	Enjoy switchback and a rocky drop-off section.
0.20	0.40	S	Cross over a footbridge and up a moderate climb.
0.20	0.60	S	Tackle another rock drop-off or choose a jug handle escape.
0.20	0.80	S	More rock drop-offs and tree crossings.
0.20	1.00	S	Trail becomes a switchback leading to a challenging rock garden.
0.20	1.20	R	After a descent, take a fork to the RIGHT.
0.20	1.40	T/L	At T-intersection, turn LEFT to loop.

Pt. to Point	Cume	Turn	Landmark
0.10	1.50	S	Trail heads to coyote rock, a boulder situated at the top of a hill; trail goes to the left in front of it.
0.10	1.60	S	Trail borders the Sprain Brook Parkway.
0.40	2.00	S	Plow through a nasty uphill rock garden and return to the other corner of the parking lot.

ॐ SLICK ROCK AND OVER THE LOG TRAIL

Trip Length:	1.60 miles
Difficulty:	Advanced
Trail Configuration:	One Way
Elevation Change:	200 feet
Trail Type:	Singletrack

Pt. to Point	Cume	Turn	Landmark
0.00	0.00	L	Enter in back far corner of the north parking lot (lot closest to the Jackson Avenue entrance) and immediately turn LEFT.
0.10	0.10	S	A short climb leads to two parallel paths, one a single track and another up onto a boulder formation (Sprain Slick Rock). A left turn will lead to a doubletrack trail down to a power line right-of-way that runs parallel to the park and to the Sprain Brook Parkway.
0.20	0.30	S	Ride carefully down a mean gnarly descent.
0.10	0.40	S	Travel through a rocky switchback climb.
0.30	0.70	S	At four-way intersection, proceed STRAIGHT.
0.10	0.80	BR	Enter a cleared area with logs for practicing trails techniques; bear RIGHT and trail re-forms to the right of a large log.
0.10	0.90	BL	Bear LEFT a fork.
0.10	1.00	S	Best of luck over a large log pile.

Pt. to Point	Cume	Turn	Landmark
0.20	1.20	S	Travel in front of a large boulder.
0.10	1.30	S	Roll through log crossings and a grassy field on level terrain.
0.30	1.60	S	Trail winds to the right and down to a doubletrack trail known as Boyce Thompson Lane.

摖 OTTER RAMBLE

Trip Length:	1.1 miles
Difficulty:	Beginner
Trail Configuration:	One Way
Elevation Change:	100 feet
Trail Type:	Singletrack

Pt. to Point	Cume	Turn	Landmark
			Starting at the interior parking lot (past the swimming pool), ride down the semi-paved Boyce Thompson Lane for about 1 mile.
0.00	0.00	R	Turn RIGHT at the yellow blazes (just before a stone bridge).
0.30	0.30	S	The trail takes you through a few easy log crossings and switchbacks. It is generally manageable and fast.
0.10	0.40	S	After a fun descent, trail merges with another trail from the right.
0.10	0.50	S	Continue past an exit to one of the interior parking lots.
0.20	0.70	S	Continue on a fast ride over level terrain and some small rock gardens.
0.40	1.10	S	Proceed down a gradual but fast slope to another interior parking lot.

Observing techniques on a descent at Sprain Ridge Park.

RIDES IN
PUTNAM COUNTY, NEW YORK

9. FAHNESTOCK
MEMORIAL STATE PARK

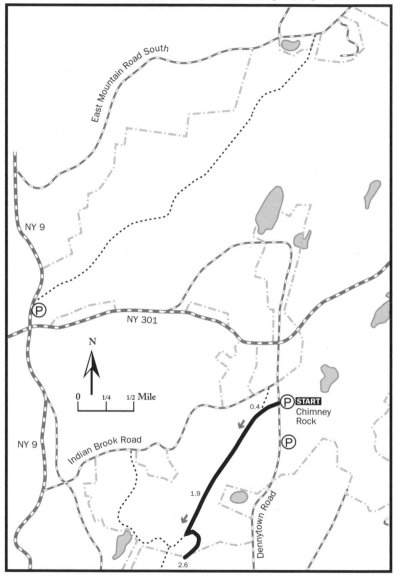

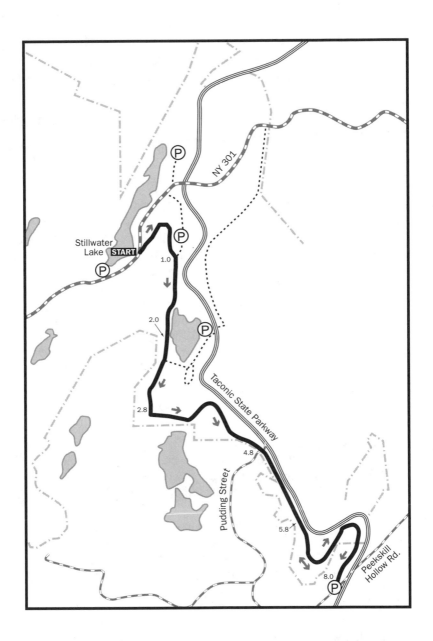

LOCATION:	Carmel, New York
DISTANCE FROM NYC:	1.5 hours (57 miles)
TRAILS DESCRIBED:	Stillwater Lake Trail;
	Chimney Rock Trail

Overview

Clarence Fahnestock Memorial State Park is a 6,500-acre park located in the highlands of Putnam County. The original 2,700 acres of the park were donated to the State of New York in 1929 by Dr. Ernest Fahnestock as a memorial to his brother. The park boasts spectacular views of the Hudson River and the Hudson Highland Range. The park actually consists of two distinct sections, each of which has its own mountain-biking trail. Both trails are included here. Note that the parking lots and trailheads are different for the two trails. The Stillwater Lake Trail begins at Pelton Pond, a man-made pond formed from the damming of a 1930 iron ore mineshaft. The Chimney Rock Trail begins near the Taconic Outdoor Education Center. The white-blazed Appalachian Trail, which is off limits to mountain bikers, weaves its way through both sections of the park. Fahnestock also has a fully equipped campsite, which you can reserve by calling (800) 456-CAMP.

Directions by Car

From the West Side (57th Street): Take the West Side Highway (9A) north, which becomes the Henry Hudson Parkway. After approximately 8 miles cross the Henry Hudson Bridge. Three miles later, the highway becomes the Saw Mill River Parkway. Continue for 2 more miles and exit at the Cross County Parkway East. Take the Cross County for approximately 2 miles and exit onto the Sprain Brook Parkway North. Stay on the Sprain Brook for approximately 13 miles and it becomes Taconic State Parkway. Continue on the Taconic for another 28 miles, and exit at 301 West (Cold Spring). At the stop sign, turn right, go over the highway, and pass the beach complex entrance on the right and the camping area entrance on the left. For the Stillwater Lake Trail, park in the Pelton Pond picnic area parking lot, which will be the next lot on the left (approximately 0.7 miles from the highway exit). For the Chimney Rock Trail, continue on 301 West past Pelton Pond for an additional 3 miles and turn left onto

Dennytown Road. Travel 0.7 miles on Dennytown to a parking lot on the left. The parking lot is situated immediately after a dirt road on the left. Alternatively, for shorter drive time to the Stillwater Lake Trail, you can exit the Taconic Parkway at Peekskill Hollow Road and follow the trail cues in reverse.

From the East Side: Take the FDR (62nd Street entrance used for mileage calculations) for 3 miles to the Willis Avenue Bridge (Exit 18). Cross the bridge and follow the signs for 87 North (Deegan Expressway).

Stay on 87 for 10 miles and exit at the Cross County Parkway East. Stay on the Cross County for 1 mile and exit onto the Sprain Brook Parkway North. Continue with West Side Directions.

Directions by Train

Note: Not recommended—the road ride from the train station to the trailhead is long and very steep—you might be exhausted before you reach the trail!

Take the Metro North Hudson Line to Cold Spring. Depart the train and ride onto Main Street, which runs perpendicular to the train tracks. Travel straight on Main Street, which becomes 301 East. Turn right either at Dennytown Road (and continue with driving directions) or the Pelton Pond Parking Lot. The two destinations are 5.3 miles and 8.3 miles from the train station, respectively.

ڴ *STILLWATER LAKE TRAIL*

Trip Length:	1.60 miles
Difficulty:	Advanced
Trail Configuration:	Out and Back
Elevation Change:	400 feet
Trail Type:	Singletrack and Doubletrack

Pt. to Point	Cume	Turn	Landmark
0.00	0.00	S	Facing away from the road, enter the park on the right-hand (Southern) side and ride south through the picnic area, toward the

Pt. to Point	Cume	Turn	Landmark
			south end of Pelton Pond. Pick up a trail marked with yellow blazes. Follow the trail along the western boundary of the pond.
0.30	0.30	L/T/L	Turn LEFT at the fork near the southern boundary of the pond. Shortly thereafter, the trail comes to a T with a precipitous drop off to the right. Turn LEFT. Walk your bike up a short rocky incline. Carefully navigate among the many roots and be careful with the large drop-off down to the water on the left.
0.10	0.40	R/BR/R	The trail will descend slightly and cross over a drainage pipe, then fork. Stay RIGHT at the fork and go up a short hill, away from the pond. This trail ends at a campsite parking area. Bear RIGHT through the lot, go onto a gravel road and make a RIGHT when the road ends.
0.20	0.60	R	Make the next RIGHT onto a gravel road with a red "Emergency Road—Do Not Block" sign on it and a "No Motor Vehicles" sign. This is the mountain bike trail. Years ago it was an unimproved county road. Now it is closed to vehicular traffic. The trail starts out as a carriage trail, then quickly becomes a gently rolling singletrack.
0.40	1.00	S	Enter a small pine forest. The trail is relatively flat at this point and not too rocky, though there are a few twists and turns to keep things interesting.
0.40	1.40	S	The trail begins a rocky descent. Be aggressive and hop right over the big boulders in the middle of the path.
0.10	1.50	S	The trail forks here with the left-hand spur leading to an overlook of Stillwater Lake. Go there to take a break and enjoy a view, otherwise stay right and keep on pedaling. As you continue, Stillwater Lake is on the left.

Pt. to Point	Cume	Turn	Landmark
0.10	1.60	S	Cross over a small stream.
0.50	2.10	S	The trail gets a little tougher here, and you'll know it when you hit a rocky climb followed by a number of short steep ascents and descents.
0.20	2.30	S	Here there is a great singletrack descent, probably the best one on the trail going this direction. Enjoy!
0.50	2.80	BL	Two large boulders are on the right side with a trail off to the right. Stay LEFT (the trail on the right leads out of the park and onto private Boy Scout land).
0.10	2.90	S	The trail crosses over a bridge and then goes through a rocky stream bed.
0.10	3.00	S	Stay STRAIGHT as you see a trail to the right.
0.10	3.10	S	Go up a steep, twisting ascent.
0.20	3.30	S	Ride through a split rock to the left and right.
0.20	3.50	S	While cranking up this hill, don't miss the spectacular boulder field off to the right.
0.20	3.70	S	The trail flattens out and leads toward the Taconic Parkway.
0.50	4.20	L	As the trail flattens out and leads toward a property boundary, turn LEFT onto a singletrack leading down to a grassy area.
0.20	4.40	L	As the trail turns gravelly and starts to incline, turn LEFT onto singletrack. (Going straight would lead to Wiccoppe Road, an alternate parking area for this trail.)
0.30	4.70	S	Enjoy a fast, rocky singletrack descent.
0.10	4.80	L/R	The trail comes to a road, Pudding Street. Turn LEFT, then make a quick RIGHT back onto a singletrack trail, alongside the Taconic Parkway.
1.00	5.80	S	After traveling along the western side of the Taconic State Parkway, the trail turns right, away from the parkway and over rolling terrain.
0.60	6.40	S	Pass a hut with a stone fireplace on the left

Pt. to Point	Cume	Turn	Landmark
			during a fun switchback descent.
0.80	7.20	S	Descent becomes steeper and trail meanders back toward the Taconic Parkway. The trail continues along the boundary of the park, through open grassy sections, with a generally flat to downward sloping grade.
0.40	7.60	S	Fast, rocky descent.
0.20	7.80	S	Trail levels off.
0.20	8.00	S	Trail ends at Peekskill Hollow Road, underneath the Taconic State Parkway overpass.

⬥ CHIMNEY ROCK TRAIL

Trip Length:	5.10 miles
Difficulty:	Intermediate
Trail Configuration:	Out and Back
Elevation Change:	220 feet
Trail Type:	Singletrack

Pt. to Point	Cume	Turn	Landmark
0.00	0.00	S	The trailhead is directly across the street from the entrance to the parking lot. Enter through the wide opening, which soon becomes singletrack and leads to a small pine forest.
0.20	0.20	R	The trail takes a 90-degree RIGHT turn. Don't go left.
0.10	0.30	S	The trail goes down a rocky descent and crosses a small steam.
0.05	0.35	T/L	The trail comes to a T-stop. Turn LEFT. At this point, the trail goes up a gradual singletrack incline.
0.35	0.70	S	Notice an intersecting trail marked with blue blazes.

Pt. to Point	Cume	Turn	Landmark
0.30	1.00	S	Continue STRAIGHT, along the flat, wide singletrack. The trees are short and the undergrowth is dense here, making for a great canopy effect in the summer. Enjoy beautiful vistas on both sides of the trail in the winter.
0.30	1.30	S	Enjoy some rolling up-and-down riding. The trail is well groomed with just enough rocks to keep the advanced rider challenged.
0.20	1.50	S	A quick uphill climb leads to a gradual downhill.
0.40	1.90	S	Notice an intersecting trail marked with red blaze. Continue STRAIGHT and immediately cross a small stream.
0.05	1.95	S	Enter a pine forest.
0.10	2.05	L	Near the end of the pine forest, make a sharp LEFT turn, almost reversing in direction.
0.20	2.25	R	Turn RIGHT at the fork, after a nice climb.
0.30	2.55	S/X	Trail ends at Chimney Rock, the remains of a house built on a ledge with breathtaking vistas of the Hudson Valley, including Bear Mountain to the left, Storm King Mountain straight ahead, and the Catskills in the distance. Take a seat, have a drink, then head back the same way.

Rolling over a technical descent.

Photo by William Schmitt

10. NINHAM MOUNTAIN

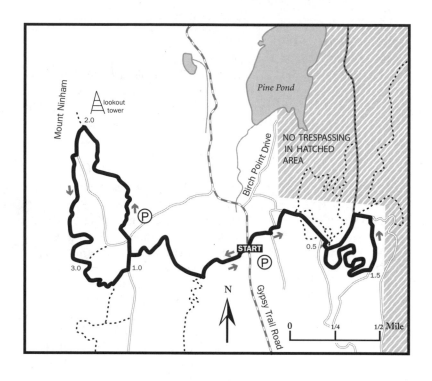

LOCATION:	Kent, New York
DISTANCE FROM NYC:	1.5 hours (60 miles)
TRAILS DESCRIBED:	Lookout Tower Loop; East Trails

Overview

Ninham Mountain Multiple Use Area is an over-1,000-acre park located in Kent, New York, in Putnam County. The park is a popular mountain-biking destination given its varied terrain, mix of fire roads and singletrack, elevation gain and shear size. Of note, as a "multiple use area," it is also open for hunting during the fall, so to be safe, check with the NY Department of Environmental Protection (www.nyc.gov/dep) to see if it is hunting season before riding at Ninham. Note also that an access permit from DEP is required to ride at Ninham. You can register and print out a permit free of charge at the web site listed above. A note of caution: much of the park borders and many of the trails cross into private land. Please do not ride beyond the posted No Trespassing signs, as there have been reports of bicycle confiscation by patrols within the private land.

Two notable attractions at Ninham are the highly technical singletrack and the lookout tower. As if the singletrack trails through boulders and rock formations sloping through varied elevations of densely wooded terrain weren't challenging enough, local trail builders have mixed in side trails with launch sites, chutes and ladder-crossings to make Ninham a true cross-"stuntry" and free-ride destination. However, this is quite an appealing destination even for the technically challenged, provided you have the aerobic capacity to slog up the carriage trail to the lookout tower. There you can climb the 102 stairs to the top of the 90 foot tower and enjoy a 360-degree view including the West Branch Reservoir, the Shawangunks and the Catskills. Built in the 1930s and refurbished in 2005, the tower is listed in the National Historic Register.

There are two parking lots at Ninham, both accessible from Gypsy Trail Road, which bisects the park. The west lot is at the end of a half mile long road off Gypsy Trail. The road has a sign reading "Ninham Mountain Multiple Use Area." The east lot (with a sign reading "Ninham Field Headquarters") is immediately off Gypsy Trail Road. Both have access to fire roads and singletrack trails. The west lot offers easier access to the trails to the lookout tower.

Directions by Car

From the West Side (57th Street): Take the West Side Highway (9A) north, which becomes the Henry Hudson Parkway. After approximately 8 miles, cross over the Henry Hudson Bridge. Three miles later, the highway becomes the Saw Mill River Parkway. Continue for 2 more miles and exit at the Cross County Parkway East. Take the Cross County for approximately 2 miles and exit onto the Sprain Brook Parkway North. Stay on the Sprain for approximately 13 miles and it becomes the Taconic State Parkway. Continue on the Taconic for another 22 miles and exit at Peekskill Hollow Road. At stop sign, turn right onto Peekskill Hollow Road. Travel 4 miles until the road ends at a stop sign. Turn right onto Route 301. Travel 4 additional miles (just before a bridge over the reservoir) and turn left onto Gypsy Trail Road. Pass the first two state forest signs and after approximately 2 miles, the east lot will be on the right with a sign reading "Ninham Field Headquarters." To park at the west lot, travel 0.4 miles further and turn left onto a road with a sign reading "Ninham Mountain Multiple Use Area." The lot is another 0.4 miles at the end of the road.

From the East Side: Take the FDR (62nd Street entrance used for mileage calculations) for 3 miles to the Willis Avenue Bridge (Exit 18). Cross the bridge and follow the signs for 87 North (Deegan Expressway). Stay on 87 for 10 miles and exit at the Cross County Parkway East. Stay on the Cross County for 1 mile and exit onto the Sprain Brook Parkway North. Continue with West Side directions.

Directions by Train

Take the Harlem Line to Brewster (52 miles; 1 hour 20 minutes). Exit the station and travel west on Route 6 (Carmel Avenue) for approximately 5 miles into the town of Carmel. Turn right onto Route 52 for 0.5 miles and then make the next left on route 301 west. Travel about 1 mile then cross the West Branch Reservoir Causeway. At the end, take a sharp right turn onto Gypsy Trail Road. Pass the first two state forest signs and after approximately 2 miles, the east lot will be on the right with a sign reading "Ninham Field Headquarters." To park at the west lot, travel 0.4 miles further and turn left onto a road with a sign reading "Ninham Mountain Multiple Use Area." The lot is another 0.4 miles at the end of the road.

☹ *LOOKOUT TOWER LOOP*

Trip Length:	(from either parking lot) 5 miles	
Difficulty:	Advanced	
Trail Configuration:	Loop	
Elevation Change:	700 feet	
Trail Type:	Singletrack and Doubletrack	

Pt. to Point	Cume	Turn	Landmark
0.00	0.00	L/R	Exit the east lot onto Gypsy Trail road, turn LEFT, and make a quick RIGHT onto a singletrack trail. If you parked in the west lot, go to mile 1.1.
0.10	0.10	S	Travel downhill to a rocky stream crossing, then a climb ensues.
0.30	0.40	S	Trail levels out but remains rocky and technical. Apparent forks in the trail are typically alternate routes, often of varying technical difficulty.
0.10	0.50	S	Short decline.
0.10	0.60	T/L	Stream crossing and a T-stop. Look right and notice a jump over the stream. Turn LEFT.
0.30	0.90	R or L	After another strenuous singletrack climb, trail splits in front of a large rock formation. Take either route.
0.10	1.00	R	Trail ends at a fire road. Turn RIGHT.
0.10	1.10	S	Enter the west parking lot. If you parked at the west lot, you can begin the ride here. Exit the lot at the other side, on the fire road that continues uphill the same direction as the paved road leading to the parking lot.
0.10	1.20	R	Turn RIGHT onto a singletrack trail, which leads uphill.
0.10	1.30	S	Cross over a stone fence.
0.10	1.40	S	Trail levels out but remains rocky.
0.10	1.50	S	Trail descends though a tight opening through rhododendron, which seem to grab at your handlebars. Trail then heads back up hill.
0.30	1.80	S	Trail levels out through a grassy area.
0.10	1.90	S	Trails ends at a fire road at the top of the

Pt. to Point	Cume	Turn	Landmark
			mountain. The radio tower facilities are straight ahead. The lookout tower is on the right. Take the time to climb all the way up to enjoy impressive 360-degree panoramic views.
0.10	2.00	L	To complete the loop, take the fire road on the LEFT and head down hill.
0.10	2.10	R	Turn RIGHT onto a singletrack marked with white blazes, heading downhill.
0.20	2.30	S	Trail levels off and parallels a stone fence on the right.
0.20	2.50	S	Mild climb to a clearing. Trail traverses slickrock.
0.20	2.70	S	Trail heads down along an enjoyable slickrock descent.
0.30	3.00	T/R	Trail ends at a T-intersection. Turn RIGHT.
0.20	3.20	S	Trail climbs gradually.
0.20	3.40	T/L	Trail ends at a T-stop. Turn LEFT.
0.10	3.50	R/L	Trail ends at a doubletrack trail with a circle to the left; turn RIGHT, then make another LEFT when that trail ends at a fire road.
0.10	3.60	R or S	You can turn RIGHT on the singletrack (same as mile 1.0 from above) and reverse course to the east lot, or continue STRAIGHT.
0.10	3.70	S	Re-enter the west lot or
0.90	4.60	S	re-enter the east lot.

🚲 *EAST TRAILS*

Trip Length:	(from east side parking lot) 3 miles
Difficulty:	Advanced
Trail Configuration:	Loop
Elevation Change:	300 feet
Trail Type:	Singletrack and Doubletrack

Pt. to Point	Cume	Turn	Landmark
0.00	0.00	S	Exit the east lot traveling away from Gypsy Trail

Pt. to Point	Cume	Turn	Landmark
			Road, past a gate and along a light colored gravel road, which narrows to a singletrack trail.
0.10	0.10	L	Follow the trail to the LEFT. There is a red-blazed singletrack on the right side into a dense stand of pine trees, offering an alternative route to mile 0.3.
0.20	0.30	S	Note a trail exiting a pine forest from the right. Continue STRAIGHT and cross an earthen dam with a pond on the right.
0.10	0.40	S	As the trail heads back into the woods and uphill, note a blue blazed singletrack trail on the left side of the carriage trail and two consecutive singletrack trails on the right.
0.10	0.50	BL	Trail forks. Stay LEFT. Note equestrian obstacles on the trail to the right.
0.10	0.60	R	The carriage trail continues up and turns to the left; turn RIGHT onto a singletrack trail to the right with a tree at the fork.
0.20	0.80	S	Encounter a challenging, quarter-mile ascent over slickrock formations.
0.30	1.10	S	Enjoy a fun 8-foot slickrock descent.
0.10	1.20	S	Tough short climb through rhododendron.
0.10	1.30	S	Challenging slickrock descent requiring a turn mid-stream.
0.10	1.40	T/L	Trail ends at T-stop. Turn LEFT. (Right turn loops back to the fork at mile 0.5.)
0.10	1.50	L	Turn LEFT with No Trespassing sign on trail to the right.
0.20	1.70	L	Turn LEFT with another No Trespassing sign on trail to the right; note another single track trail on the right.
0.10	1.80	BL	Stay LEFT at the fork.
0.10	1.90	S	Pass a singletrack trail on right as carriage trail starts to descend.
0.10	2.00	S	Loop returns to marker at 0.6 from the opposite direction.
0.20	2.20	S	Cross the earthen dam and travel up the carriage trail on the other side.
0.30	2.50	BR	Follow the trail RIGHT and out of the woods.
0.10	2.60	S	Return to the east lot.

RIDES IN
LONG ISLAND

11. CALVERTON MOUNTAIN BIKE TRAIL

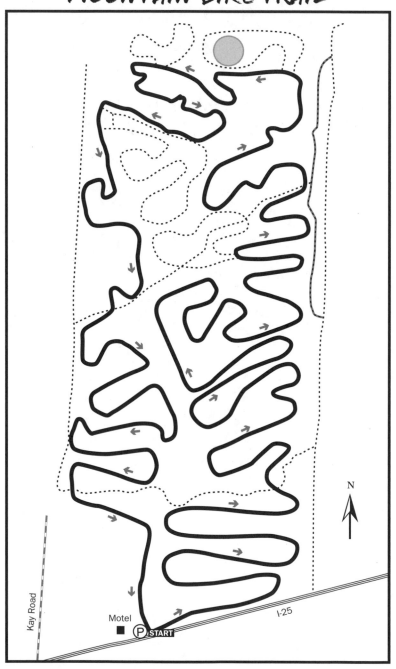

LOCATION:	Calverton, New York
DISTANCE FROM NYC:	1.5 hours (67 miles)
TRAILS DESCRIBED:	Calverton Mountain Bike Trail
DIFFICULTY LEVEL:	Beginner

Overview

The Calverton Mountain Bike Trail is located adjacent to the Calverton National Cemetery in Suffolk County, Long Island. The trailhead is on Route 25. The Calverton MTB trail offers a great beginner mountain bike experience, with minimal elevation gain and a tight layout that makes it easy to find your way. The trail in the park is set up as a one-way, 9-mile loop. However, there are four additional spur loops that offer more technical riding that attracts advanced riders as well. The trail is situated on NYS Dept. of Environmental Conservation land and as such a DEC permit is required.

Directions by Car

From the East Side: Take the midtown tunnel (entrance on 2nd Avenue between 36th and 37th streets) out of Manhattan, traveling East on Interstate 495. Stay on 495 for approximately 59 miles until Exit 68 North. Take William Floyd Parkway North for 4 miles. Turn right onto Route 25 East and travel 3.5 miles. Parking lot is on the left, just after a motel.

12. CATHEDRAL PINES COUNTY PARK

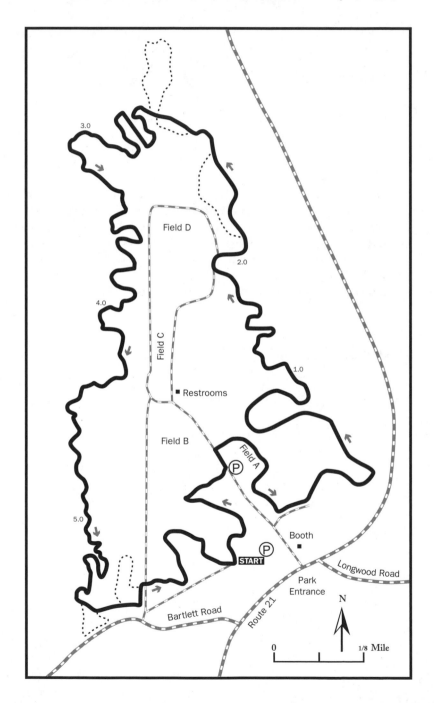

Field D

3.0

2.0

Field C

4.0

1.0

■ Restrooms

Field B

Field A

Ⓟ

5.0

Ⓟ

Booth ■

START Ⓟ

Longwood Road

Park
Entrance

Bartlett Road

Route 21

N

0   1/8 Mile

LOCATION:	Middle Island, New York
DISTANCE FROM NYC:	1.5 hour (70 miles)
TRAILS DESCRIBED:	Cathedral Pines Mountain Bike Trail
DIFFICULTY LEVEL:	Beginner

Overview

This 320-acre site is situated along the headwaters of the Carmans River. Adjacent to Cathedral Pines Park is Prosser Pines Nature Preserve, which features a majestic stand of white pines planted in 1812. Park near the back of the main parking lot. You will see a large sign with a trail map on it and a wide trail with a gate blocking vehicular traffic. The mountain-biking trail access is just beyond the gate.

Directions by Car

Take the midtown tunnel (entrance on 2nd Avenue between 36th and 37th streets) out of Manhattan, traveling east on Interstate 495. Stay on 495 for approximately 60 miles until Exit 66 north (Sills Road). Turn left at the light. Bear left at flashing light (Middle Island/Yaphank Road). Park is on your left just before traffic light at Longwood Road.

Description

The Cathedral Pines Mountain Biking Trail is a well-groomed singletrack 6-mile one-way loop with an elevation change of 150 feet. It begins just beyond the gate at the back of the main parking lot. The main loop is fairly easy fast singletrack, but there are five more technical off-shoot trails for more experienced riders.

13. EASTPORT
MOUNTAIN BIKE TRAIL

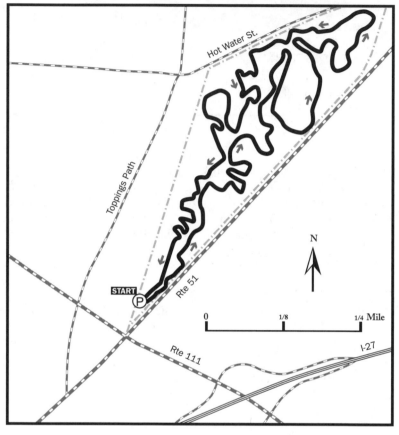

LOCATION:	Eastport, New York
DISTANCE FROM NYC:	1.5 hours (68 miles)
TRAILS DESCRIBED:	Eastport Mountain Bike Trail
DIFFICULTY LEVEL:	9 miles of Beginner/ Intermediate Singletrack

Overview

The Eastport Mountain Bike Trail is in a triangle-shaped sliver of land adjacent to Route 51 in Suffolk County, Long Island. The trailhead is near the intersection of Route 111 and Route 51. The Eastport MTB trail offers a great beginner mountain bike experience, with minimal elevation gain in a small park of fields and forest where it is difficult to get lost. The trail in the park is set up as a one-way, 9-mile loop. The trail is situated on NYS Dept. of Environmental Conservation land and as such a DEC permit is required.

Directions by Car

From the East Side: Take the midtown tunnel (entrance on 2nd Avenue between 36th and 37th streets) out of Manhattan, traveling East on Interstate 495. Stay on 495 for approximately 64 miles until Exit 70 (Manorville/Eastport). At the exit, turn right and proceed South on Route 111 (*Note*: not the route 111 at Exit 56) for approximately 4 miles until East Moriches/Riverhead Road East. At the first crossover, make a U-turn and the parking lot will be on the right, before the overpass.

14. GLACIER RIDGE MOUNTAIN BIKE TRAIL

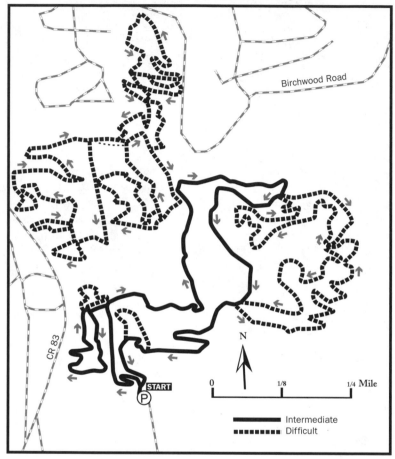

Birchwood Road

CR 83

START

P

N

0   1/8   1/4 Mile

———— Intermediate
•••••••• Difficult

LOCATION:	Farmingville, New York
DISTANCE FROM NYC:	1.2 hours (54 miles)
TRAILS DESCRIBED:	Glacier Ridge Mountain Bike Trail
DIFFICULTY LEVEL:	11 miles of Intermediate Singletrack

Overview

The Glacier Ridge Mountain Bike Trail is a collection of trails in a park adjacent to CR83 in Suffolk County, Long Island. The trailhead is located at the Brookhaven Town Hall. Glacier Ridge is located in a nature preserve along the highest ridge in Long Island. It offers a well diversified, somewhat hilly (for Long Island) mountain bike experience along 11 miles of one-way singletrack coupled with over 3 miles of additional spur loops that offer more technical riding for advanced riders. There are also multiple fire roads throughout the park with signage back to the parking lot. Total elevation change is as much as 200 feet in some sections, with peaks of 210-250 feet.

Directions by Car

From the East Side: Take the midtown tunnel (entrance on 2nd Avenue between 36th and 37th streets) out of Manhattan, traveling East on Interstate 495. Stay on 495 for approximately 53 miles until Exit 63. Take Ocean Avenue (Route 83) north for 1 mile. Turn right onto Bicycle Path Road for 0.25 mile, then turn left onto Independence Hill Drive at the Town of Brookhaven Town Hall. Proceed toward the end and park near the Wind Mill. Trailhead is on the left side of a low white building.

15. HITHER HILLS STATE PARK

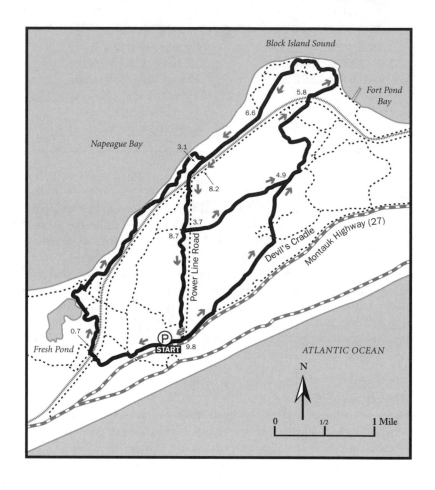

LOCATION:	Montauk, New York
DISTANCE FROM NYC:	2.75 hours (109 miles)
TRAILS DESCRIBED:	Hither Woods Preserve;
	Napeague Bay;
	The Devil's Cradle

Overview

Hither Hills is a 1,755-acre park located between Amagansett and Montauk on eastern Long Island. Vegetation in the park consists of Russian olive trees, oak, and pine together with a tangled undergrowth of rhododendron and various wild grapes and berries. As its name indicates, the park is uncharacteristically hilly considering its location. However, from a mountain biker's perspective, the rolling hills in a savannah setting are not only easily manageable compared to inland mountain biking, but they also provide for some breathtaking vistas, especially atop the cliffs along the Napeague Bay. Be careful not to stray off the trails. The park's many thorn bushes can easily puncture a tire and cause a flat. Hither Hills is a multi-use park with a 165-site campground located adjacent to the Atlantic Ocean. There is also a large public beach within minutes of the trails. Make sure to take advantage of this! There is nothing like a surf-and-turf adventure of working up a sweat on the trails of Hither Hills followed by a refreshing dip in the Atlantic. Our mountain-biking buddies in Boulder can't do that!

Directions by Car

Take the midtown tunnel (entrance on 2nd Avenue between 36th and 37th streets) out of Manhattan, traveling east on Interstate 495. Stay on 495 for approximately 64 miles until Exit 70 (Manorville/Eastport). At the exit, turn right and proceed south on Route 111 (*Note*: not the Route 111 at Exit 56) for approximately 5 miles. Then go east on Highway 27 for approximately 39 miles, through all of the Hamptons and Amagansett, until the road forks. Stay left at the fork, on 27. (Old Montauk Highway is the road on the right fork.) Continue on 27 for 1 more mile, passing the Hither Hills entrance on the right, and turn left into the Overlook parking area.

Directions by Train

Take the LIRR to Montauk. At the train station, make a right onto Edgemere Road. Proceed on Edgemere for 1 mile until it comes to a circle. Make a right at the circle and then the next right onto Montauk Highway (Route 27). Continue west on 27 for about 4 miles and turn right into the Overlook parking area.

ڶڶ *HITHER WOODS PRESERVE*

Trip Length:	9.80 miles
Difficulty:	Intermediate
Trail Configuration:	Figure 8
Elevation Change:	150 feet
Trail Type:	Singletrack

Pt. to Point	Cume	Turn	Landmark
0.00	0.00	R/L/S	On the left side of the parking lot (facing the descriptive sign), turn RIGHT, ride for a short distance, then make a quick LEFT down a short hill. At the three-way fork, go STRAIGHT on a singletrack trail, which quickly descends through a narrow S-turn into the woods. This trail continues to descend and goes through some open sandy patches. Keep heading straight, avoiding any turn-offs that seem like trails.
0.30	0.30	R/L	The singletrack abruptly ends at a sandy doubletrack dirt road. Turn RIGHT. The road quickly comes to a fork. Stay LEFT. Continue on this trail, up a short hill, until it ends at a T-stop.
0.30	0.60	T/R/L	Turn RIGHT at the T-stop. This is Old Tar Road (notice the remnants of an asphalt top). Quickly make the next LEFT that leads to the railroad. Check for trains, then proceed directly over the tracks into a small opening in the woods on the other side of the tracks.

Pt. to Point	Cume	Turn	Landmark
0.10	0.70	R/S	Once in the forest, make the first RIGHT onto a singletrack trail that runs parallel to the railroad track. Notice a spur road off to the right. Ignore it and continue STRAIGHT.
0.40	1.10	R	The trail bears to the RIGHT with some small noticeable trails straight and off to the left. These trails lead to Fresh Pond, which is two minutes away by foot. If you go to take a peek, don't take your bike.
0.10	1.20	S/R/T/S	Bearing to the right and uphill, continue STRAIGHT on the main trail, which ends on a downgrade where there are a few large boulders. Make a RIGHT onto the dirt road beyond the boulders. The trail forks at one point but quickly comes back together and shortly thereafter comes to a T-intersection. (On the right there is a railroad crossing and a stop sign.) Continue STRAIGHT across the intersection, where the trail continues up on an embankment.
0.10	1.30	S	Enjoy this rolling singletrack for about a half mile, then look to the left to observe Napeague Bay. Continue STRAIGHT on the singletrack.
0.80	2.10	S	The trail begins a steep descent with a sharp left at the bottom, and shortly thereafter merges with another trail from the left. Continuing STRAIGHT, the trail heads toward the bay.
0.10	2.20	R	With the bay in view, make a RIGHT at the stake and ride along the trail with the bay on the left.
0.20	2.40	S	Continuing STRAIGHT, re-enter the forest and come to two consecutive steep, sandy uphills. Here you must walk your bike.
0.50	2.90	S	Notice a short spur road off to the left,

Pt. to Point	Cume	Turn	Landmark
			with a great view of the bay. Back on the main route, continue STRAIGHT down a steep hill.
0.20	3.10	R	Trail ends at a T-stop. Turn RIGHT.
0.10	3.20	S	Trail ends at railroad tracks. Cross over and head STRAIGHT toward a narrow uphill trail on the other side of the tracks, to the left of a birdhouse. This quickly dumps onto Old North Road, a doubletrack trail.
0.10	3.30	S/R/BL	There is a five-way intersection. Old Tar Road is on the right. Continue STRAIGHT on Old North Road. After crossing over Old Tar Road, stay RIGHT at the first fork (the road to the left connects with a sandy dirt road called Powerline Road). At the next fork, bear LEFT onto a narrow singletrack trail. This very narrow singletrack is rather hilly, with low-lying shrubbery on either side of the trail.
0.40	3.70	L	At an intersection with a grassy doubletrack road, turn LEFT. This is Flaggy Hole Road. Immediately cross Powerline Road and continue along Flaggy Hole, a relatively flat, grassy doubletrack that eventually narrows to singletrack.
1.00	4.70	S	There is a road off to the right. Continue going STRAIGHT on what is now a singletrack trail. As the trail begins to descend, look for a trail to the left.
0.20	4.90	L	Make a sharp LEFT turn, which will lead into a doubletrack descent.
0.20	5.10	L	Make a LEFT at the fork and enjoy some challenging downhill singletrack.
0.50	5.60	S	Cross over a trail going diagonally from left to right and continue STRAIGHT. Ignore two right side spur roads.
0.20	5.80	S	Cross over Powerline Road, then cross over the railroad tracks and continue

Pt. to Point	Cume	Turn	Landmark
			STRAIGHT on enjoyable downhill singletrack to a T-stop with an excellent view of Fort Pond Bay.
0.30	6.10	**L/S**	Turn LEFT onto a sandy dirt road (Old North Road). Go up the hill and keep going STRAIGHT on the doubletrack. Ignore three consecutive grassy right side turn-offs.
0.50	6.60	**BR**	At the fork, bear RIGHT on the sandy road.
0.10	6.70	**L**	Turn LEFT when the trail hits Napeague Bay. Enjoy some excellent singletrack along the bay.
0.30	7.00	**T/L**	Trail ends at T-stop. Turn LEFT.
0.10	7.10	**T/R**	This ends at T-stop. Turn RIGHT onto Old North Road.
0.80	7.90	**S**	Continuing on Old North Road, there is a road to the right. Stay STRAIGHT.
0.20	8.10	**BL**	The road will fork. Stay LEFT.
0.10	8.20	**S**	Trail ends at railroad tracks (same place as mile 3.2). As before, cross over and head STRAIGHT toward a narrow uphill trail on the other side of the tracks. This quickly dumps onto Old North Road, a doubletrack trail.
0.10	8.30	**S/R/BL**	This is a five-way intersection. Old Tar Road is on the right. Continue STRAIGHT on Old North Road. After crossing over Old Tar Road, stay RIGHT at the first fork (the road to the left connects with a sandy dirt road called Powerline Road). At the next fork, bear LEFT onto a narrow singletrack trail.
0.40	8.70	**S**	The singletrack intersects a grassy doubletrack road, Flaggy Hole Road. Continue STRAIGHT, crossing over Flaggy Hole Road.
0.10	8.80	**S**	Continuing STRAIGHT, there is a steep hill where you may have to walk your bike.

Pt. to Point	Cume	Turn	Landmark
			Then enjoy some nice, tight singletrack over rolling hills.
0.60	9.40	S	Continuing STRAIGHT, there is another steep uphill.
0.30	9.70	S/R	Staying STRAIGHT, come out into the open and Powerline Road is on the left and Highway 27 is straight ahead. Turn RIGHT at a birdhouse onto singletrack.
0.10	9.80	S	The trail ends at Overlook.

🚲 NAPEAGUE BAY

Trip Length:	4.80 miles
Difficulty:	Intermediate
Trail Configuration:	Loop
Elevation Change:	100 feet
Trail Type:	Singletrack

Pt. to Point	Cume	Turn	Landmark
0.00	0.0	R/L/S/S	On the left side of the parking lot (facing the descriptive sign), turn RIGHT, ride for a short distance, then make a quick LEFT down a short hill. At the three-way fork, go STRAIGHT on a singletrack trail, which quickly descends through a narrow S-turn into the woods. This trail continues to descend and goes through some open sandy patches. Keep heading STRAIGHT, avoiding any turn-offs that seem like trails.
0.30	0.30	R/L	The singletrack abruptly ends at a sandy doubletrack dirt road. Turn RIGHT. The road quickly comes to a fork. Stay LEFT. Continue on this trail, up a short hill, until it ends at a T-stop.
0.30	0.60	T/R/L	Turn RIGHT at the T-stop. This is Old Tar Road (notice the remnants of an asphalt

Pt. to Point	Cume	Turn	Landmark
			top). Quickly make the next LEFT that leads to the railroad. Check for trains, then proceed directly over the tracks into a small opening in the woods on the other side of the tracks.
0.10	0.70	R/S	Once in the forest, make the first RIGHT onto a singletrack trail that runs parallel to the railroad track. Notice a spur road off to the right. Ignore it and continue STRAIGHT.
0.40	1.10	BR	The trail bears to the RIGHT with some small noticeable trails straight and off to the left. There trails lead to Fresh Pond, which is two minutes away by foot. If you go to take a peek, don't take your bike.
0.10	1.20	S/R/T/S	Bearing to the right and uphill, continue STRAIGHT on the main trail, which ends on a downgrade where there are a few large boulders. Make a RIGHT onto the dirt road beyond the boulders. The trail forks at one point but quickly comes back together and shortly thereafter comes to a T-intersection. (On the right there is a railroad crossing and a stop sign.) Continue STRAIGHT across the intersection, where the trail continues up on an embankment.
0.10	1.30	S	Enjoy this rolling singletrack for about a half mile, then look to the left to observe Napeague Bay. Continue STRAIGHT on the singletrack.
0.80	2.10	S	The trail begins a steep descent with a sharp left at the bottom, and shortly thereafter merges with another trail from the left. Continuing STRAIGHT, the trail heads toward the bay.
0.10	2.20	R	With the bay in view, make a RIGHT at the stake and ride along the trail with the bay on the left.

Pt. to Point	Cume	Turn	Landmark
0.20	2.40	S	Continuing STRAIGHT, re-enter the forest and come to two consecutive steep, sandy uphills. Here you must walk your bike.
0.50	2.90	S	Notice a short spur road off to the left, with a great view of the bay. Back on the main route, continue STRAIGHT down a steep hill.
0.20	3.10	T/R	Trail ends at a T-stop. Turn RIGHT.
0.10	3.20	S	Trail ends at railroad tracks. Cross over and head STRAIGHT toward a narrow uphill trail on the other side of the tracks, to the left of a birdhouse. This quickly dumps onto Old North Road, a doubletrack trail.
0.10	3.30	S/R/BL	There is a five-way intersection. Old Tar Road is on the right. Continue STRAIGHT on Old North Road. After crossing over Old Tar Road, stay RIGHT at the first fork (the road to the left connects with a sandy dirt road called Powerline Road). At the next fork, bear LEFT onto a narrow singletrack trail. This very narrow singletrack is rather hilly, with low-lying shrubbery on either side of the trail.
0.40	3.70	S	The singletrack intersects with a grassy doubletrack road, Flaggy Hole Road. Continue STRAIGHT, crossing over Flaggy Hole Road.
0.1	3.80	S	Continuing STRAIGHT, there is a steep hill where you may have to walk your bike. Then enjoy some nice, tight singletrack over rolling hills.
0.60	4.40	S	Continuing STRAIGHT, there is another steep uphill.
0.30	4.70	S/R	Staying STRAIGHT, come out into the open and Powerline Road is on the left and Highway 27 is straight ahead. Turn RIGHT at a birdhouse onto singletrack.
0.10	4.80	S	The trail ends at Overlook.

🚲 *THE DEVIL'S CRADLE*

Trip Length:	7.00 miles
Difficulty:	Intermediate
Trail Configuration:	Loop
Elevation Change:	120 feet
Trail Type:	Singletrack

Pt. to Point	Cume	Turn	Landmark
0.00	0.00	S	Park at Overlook and enter near the sign in the middle of the parking lot. The trail begins as narrow singletrack.
0.20	0.20	S	The trail comes to an uphill grade at an intersection with a trail to the left and a birdhouse on the right. Continue STRAIGHT, crossing over Powerline Road, onto a rather flat trail that runs parallel to Highway 27.
0.10	0.30	S	Continue STRAIGHT. Notice and ignore a path off to the left.
0.10	0.50	L	Turn LEFT onto a singletrack trail.
0.60	1.10	S	Continue STRAIGHT on picturesque singletrack with an impressive canopy of vegetation above the trail. Notice split rock on the right. Ahead of the rock and to the right is the Devil's Cradle depression.
0.30	1.40	S/R	The trail ends at a grassy field. Continue STRAIGHT and join up with another trail entering the field form the right. Stay RIGHT at the fork and continue on this trail as it goes back into the woods. The trail will eventually lead downhill to a T-intersection.
0.50	1.90	T/R	At T-intersection, turn RIGHT and continue on what is now a singletrack trail. As the trail begins to descend, look for a trail to the left.
0.20	2.10	L	Make a sharp LEFT turn, which leads into a doubletrack descent.

Pt. to Point	Cume	Turn	Landmark
0.20	2.30	L	Make a LEFT at the fork and enjoy some challenging downhill singletrack.
0.50	2.80	S	Cross over a trail going diagonally from left to right and continue STRAIGHT. Ignore two right side spur roads.
0.20	3.00	S/T	Cross over Powerline Road, then cross over the railroad tracks and continue STRAIGHT on enjoyable downhill singletrack to a T-stop with an excellent view of Fort Pond Bay.
0.30	3.30	L/S	Turn LEFT onto a sandy dirt road (Old North Road). Go up the hill and keep going STRAIGHT on the doubletrack. Ignore three consecutive grassy right side turn-offs.
0.50	3.80	BR	At the fork, bear RIGHT on the sandy road.
0.10	3.90	L	Turn LEFT when the trail hits Napeague Bay. Enjoy some excellent singletrack along the bay.
0.30	4.20	T/L	Trail ends at T-stop. Turn LEFT.
0.10	4.30	T/R	This ends at T-stop. Turn RIGHT onto Old North Road.
0.80	5.10	S	Continuing on Old North Road, there is a road to the right. Stay STRAIGHT.
0.20	5.30	BL	The road will fork. Stay LEFT.
0.10	5.40	S	Trail ends at railroad tracks. Cross over and head STRAIGHT toward a narrow uphill trail on the other side of the tracks, to the left of a birdhouse. This quickly dumps onto Old North Road, a doubletrack trail.
0.10	5.50	S/R/BL	There is a five-way intersection. Old Tar Road is on the right. Continue STRAIGHT on Old North Road. After crossing over Old Tar Road, stay RIGHT at the first fork (the road to the left connects with a sandy dirt road called Powerline Road). At the next fork, bear LEFT onto a narrow singletrack trail. This very narrow

Pt. to Point	Cume	Turn	Landmark
			singletrack is rather hilly, with low-lying shrubbery on either side of the trail.
0.40	5.90	S	The singletrack intersects a grassy doubletrack road, Flaggy Hole Road. Continue STRAIGHT, crossing over Flaggy Hole Road.
0.10	6.00	S	Continuing STRAIGHT, there is a steep hill where you may have to walk your bike. Then enjoy some nice, tight singletrack over rolling hills.
0.60	6.60	S	Continuing STRAIGHT, there is another steep uphill.
0.30	6.90	S/R	Staying STRAIGHT, come out into the open and Powerline Road is on the left and Highway 27 is straight ahead. Turn RIGHT at a birdhouse onto singletrack.
0.10	7.00	S	The trail ends at Overlook.

A trail along the bay at Hither Hills.

Photo by Jennifer Sendek

16. NORTHWEST AREA

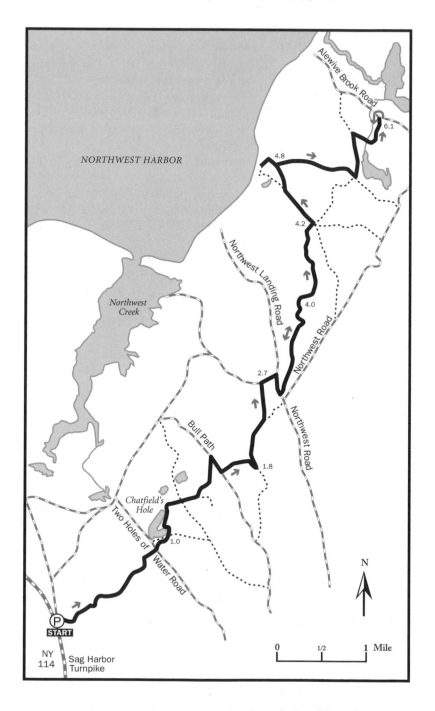

NORTHWEST HARBOR

Alewive Brook Road

6.1

4.8

4.2

Northwest Landing Road

4.0

Northwest Creek

2.7

Northwest Road

Bull Path

1.8

Chatfield's Hole

Two Holes of Water Road

1.0

START

P

NY 114

Sag Harbor Turnpike

N

0   1/2   1 Mile

LOCATION:	East Hampton, New York
DISTANCE FROM NYC:	2.5 hours (100 miles)
TRAILS DESCRIBED:	The Northwest Path

Overview

This well-groomed singletrack trail goes through rolling hills in a predominantly pine forest. The trail starts north of the town of East Hampton and ironically heads in a northeasterly directions toward Cedar Point County Park, a park with a campsite overlooking Gardiners Bay. The ride is smooth as a result of a blanket of pine needles protecting most of the trail from rocks and other obstacles. There is relatively sparse undergrowth compared to other trails on eastern Long Island. This allows better visibility and more room to maneuver. However, the trail's numerous twists and turns will challenge even the experienced mountain biker. There are a number of spur trails to explore as well, which are noted in the trail description;. However, most of these trails end at roads or the Northwest Harbor, and are not "through trails."

Directions by Car

Take the midtown tunnel (entrance on 2nd Avenue between 36th and 37th streets) out of Manhattan, traveling east on Interstate 495. Stay on 495 for approximately 64 miles until Exit 70 (Manorville/Eastport). At the exit, turn right and proceed south on Route 111 (*Note*: not the Route 111 at Exit 56) for approximately 5 miles. Then go east on Highway 27 for approximately 28 miles, through Hampton Bays, Southampton, and Bridgehampton. Once in the Village of East Hampton, make a left onto Stephen Hands Path. This left appears about half a mile after the sign "Village of East Hampton." Take Stephen Hands Path for 1 mile, then turn left onto 114 North-Sag Harbor Turnpike. Drive 1.9 miles and turn right onto a dirt road/parking lot. It is the first right turn after Whooping Hollow Road and it is opposite #558.

Directions by Train

Take the Long Island Railroad to East Hampton. Depart the train and turn right onto Railroad Avenue, then the next right onto Cooper then the next left onto Newtown Lane. Continue on this road for approximately 1.5

miles as it doglegs right and turns into Long Lane. Then turn left onto Stephen Hands Path and then the next immediate right onto 114 North-Sag Harbor Turnpike. Continue with driving directions.

🚲 *THE NORTHWEST PATH*

Trip Length:	12.20 miles
Difficulty:	Intermediate
Trail Configuration:	Out and Back
Elevation Change:	70 feet
Trail Type:	Singletrack

Pt. to Point	Cume	Turn	Landmark
0.00	0.00	S	Enter the trail at the back of the parking area. The trail runs perpendicular to Route 114 and is marked by yellow triangles.
0.10	0.10	BL	At the fork, bear LEFT following yellow triangles.
0.40	0.50	S	The trail becomes steep, then gradually descends through a few tricky sandy patches.
0.40	0.90	S	Cross over the road (Two Holes of Water Road).
0.10	1.00	BL/R/L	Bear LEFT at the fork and travel down a steep slope. Make a quick RIGHT at the bottom followed by a quick LEFT through a sandy section.
0.10	1.10	BR	Bear RIGHT at the fork. A pond, Chatfield's Hole, appears on the left.
0.30	1.40	S	Cross over an intersecting trail.
0.10	1.50	S	Trail winds right and crosses over another intersecting trail.
0.20	1.70	S	Notice a driveway on the right that is parallel to the trail.
0.10	1.80	R/L	Trail stops at a road (Bull Path). Turn RIGHT onto Bull Path then quickly turn LEFT back onto the singletrack marked by a yellow triangle.
0.10	1.90	S	Follow the trail markers as the trail winds to the left.

Pt. to Point	Cume	Turn	Landmark
0.30	2.20	S	Cross and intersecting trail. Follow "all bikes" sign.
0.30	2.50	S	Pass a house on the left, then cross a driveway.
0.20	2.70	R	Trail ends at a road, Northwest Landing Road. Turn RIGHT.
0.20	2.90	L	Immediately after the fork, turn LEFT back into the woods onto a doubletrack trail marked by two small posts.
0.10	3.00	L/S	Quickly turn LEFT back onto singletrack. Continue STRAIGHT along the rolling singletrack.
1.00	4.00	S	Pass a boulder perched on a look-out spot on the left.
0.20	4.20	T/L	Come to a T-intersection. Turn LEFT. (A RIGHT followed by two quick LEFT turns is a shortcut to mike marker 5.5.)
0.30	4.50	BR	Bear RIGHT at fork.
0.30/0.50	4.80/5.00	S/R	At intersection, eventually turn RIGHT onto doubletrack trail, but first continue STRAIGHT for 0.1 miles to a landing with a great view of Northwest Harbor.
0.70/0.50	5.50	L	At four-way intersection, turn LEFT off of doubletrack (straight leads to Northwest Road).
0.30	5.80	R	Make a sharp RIGHT at a triangular intersection. Follow yellow triangles.
0.10	5.90	L/L	Cross bridge over a small creek. Turn LEFT at the fork then LEFT again.
0.20	6.10	R/L	Trail ends at a road, Alewive Brook Road. At this point, you can either head back or continue to Cedar Point Park. To get to Cedar Point Park, turn RIGHT on Alewive Brook Road and make a LEFT onto Cedar Point Road (mile 6.4). Travel 0.3 miles and obtain a map at the park office. There is a short singletrack trail that begins just beyond the park office that leads to a seaside trail with fabulous ocean views atop dramatic bluffs.

17. ROCKY POINT MOUNTAIN BIKE TRAIL

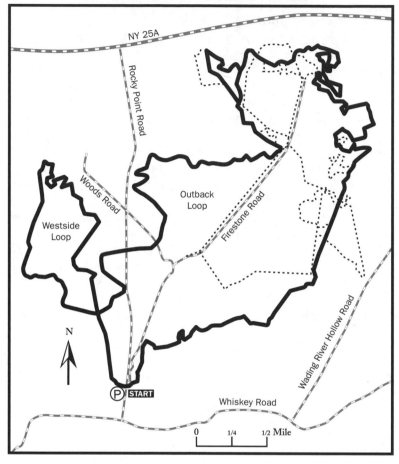

NY 25A

Rocky Point Road

Woods Road

Outback Loop

Firestone Road

Westside Loop

Wading River Hollow Road

N

START

Whiskey Road

0   1/4   1/2 Mile

LOCATION:	Rocky Point, New York
DISTANCE FROM NYC:	1.5 hours (68 miles)
TRAILS DESCRIBED:	Rocky Point Mountain Bike Trail
DIFFICULTY LEVEL:	Beginner/Intermediate

Overview

The Rocky Point Mountain Bike Trail is a collection of trails in a park adjacent to Route 25A in Suffolk County, Long Island. Trailheads are located on Rocky Point Road as well as along route 25A. The Rocky Point MTB trail offers a well diversified, generally flat mountain bike experience along the main 13-mile loop coupled with over 4 miles of additional spur loops that offer more technical riding for advanced riders. A wide bail-out route (Firestone Road) essentially bisects the park. The trail is situated on NYS Dept. of Environmental Conservation land and as such a DEC permit is required.

Directions by Car

From the East Side: Take the midtown tunnel (entrance on 2nd Avenue between 36th and 37th streets) out of Manhattan, traveling east on Interstate 495. Stay on 495 for approximately 59 miles until Exit 68 North. Take William Floyd Parkway North 5 miles. Turn left on Whiskey Road. After 4 miles, turn right on Rocky Point Road. Parking lot is on the left. If the lot is full, continue north 1 mile on Rocky Point Road and turn right on Route 25A. After 0.5 miles, bear right and there are two additional parking areas on the right.

18. STILLWELL WOODS AND NASSAU/ SUFFOLK GREENBELT TRAILS

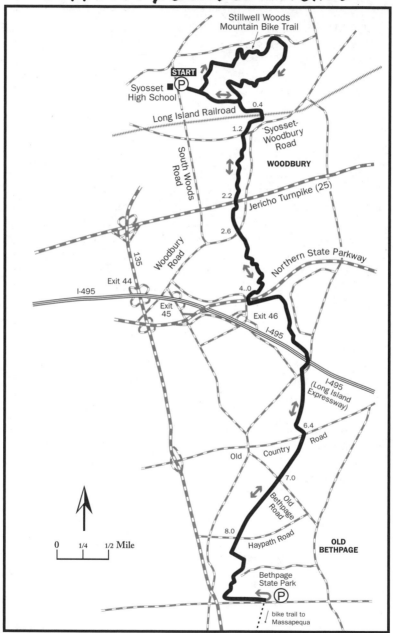

Stillwell Woods
Mountain Bike Trail

START
P

Syosset
High School

Long Island Railroad   0.4

1.2   Syosset-
Woodbury
Road

WOODBURY

South Woods Road

2.2   Jericho Turnpike (25)

2.6

Woodbury Road   Northern State Parkway

135

Exit 44   4..0

I-495

Exit 45

Exit 46

I-495

I-495
(Long Island
Expressway)

6.4   Road

Old   Country

7.0

Old Bethpage Road

8.0   Haypath Road

OLD
BETHPAGE

Bethpage
State Park
P

bike trail to
Massapequa

0   1/4   1/2 Mile

LOCATION:	Syosset, New York
DISTANCE FROM NYC:	1 hour (30 miles)
TRAILS DESCRIBED:	Stillwell Woods Mountain Bike Trail; Nassau-Suffolk Greenbelt Trail

Overview

Stillwell Woods is a 4.5 mile, one-way mountain-biking loop in a small park near the Nassau-Suffolk county line. The mountain-biking loop encounters heavy traffic and therefore it is important to follow the instructions at the entrance of the loop and only travel in the direction posted. While not particularly strenuous or rocky, Stillwell Woods offers tight singletrack with frequent twists and turns. The trail itself is smooth with occasional roots and few large rocks or boulders. Stillwell Woods also provides an entry point to the mountain-biking section of the Nassau-Suffolk Greenbelt trail, a relatively flat north/south trail along the county line. Also heavily used, the Greenbelt trail has separate sections for hiking and mountain biking; be sure to follow the signs and remain on the dedicated mountain-biking trail.

Directions by Car

Take the midtown tunnel (entrance on 2nd Avenue between 36th and 37th streets) out of Manhattan, traveling east on Interstate 495. Stay on 495 for approximately 27 miles until Exit 44 (135 North). At the exit, proceed north on Route 135 toward Syosset for approximately 1 mile. Then go east on Highway 25 (Jericho Turnpike) for approximately 1 mile. At the third light, turn left onto South Woods Road. Proceed 1.3 miles until you see Stillwell Woods on the right (opposite Syosset High School). Park in the back of the parking lot.

Directions by Train

Take the LIRR to Syosset. At the train station, make a right off the platform and a left onto Jackson Avenue. Travel 1 mile south and turn left onto Jericho Turnpike (Highway 25). Go east on Jericho Turnpike for approximately 1 mile. Turn left onto South Woods Road. Proceed 1.3 miles until you see Stillwell Woods on the right (opposite Syosset High School).

ठ्ठ *STILLWELL WOODS MOUNTAIN BIKE TRAIL*

Trip Length:	4.50 miles
Difficulty:	Intermediate
Trail Configuration:	Loop
Elevation Change:	50 feet
Trail Type:	Singletrack

Pt. to Point	Cume	Turn	Landmark
0.00	0.00	L	Enter the trail at the back of the parking lot and turn LEFT at the Stillwell Woods Mountain Bike Trail sign. Read the information on the sign and note that the trail is one way, marked with white triangles.
0.30	0.30	S	Trail enters a pine forest.
0.20	0.50	T/L	Trail comes out of the woods and comes to a T-intersection. Turn LEFT and follow the triangle markings straight ahead.
0.20	0.70	BR	Bear RIGHT back into the woods. Enjoy a bumpy descent.
0.20	0.90	BR/L/L	Bear RIGHT at the bottom then LEFT up a hill and LEFT at the top of the hill leading to some winding singletrack.
0.20	1.10	BL	Bear LEFT at the fork.
0.20	1.30	S	Encounter a small rock garden after a brief descent.
0.10	1.40	BR/L/L/L	Bear RIGHT onto a stone path, then make the next LEFT back onto singletrack, then two quick LEFT turns.
0.20	1.60	BR	Bear RIGHT as the trail winds downhill.
0.10	1.70	BL	Bear LEFT at fork.
0.20	1.90	S	Go down a steep descent, cross over a gully, and proceed STRAIGHT through a number of criss-crossing trails. Resist the tendency of your bike to bear left up a slope (sign indicates "wrong way").
0.10	2.00	S	Cross over an intersecting path.
0.20	2.20	BR	Bear RIGHT.
0.10	2.30	T/BR/S	Bear RIGHT again at T-intersection, then

Pt. to Point	Cume	Turn	Landmark
			proceed STRAIGHT up a hill, avoiding sandy path on left.
0.10	2.40	R	Turn RIGHT at the next intersection.
0.20	2.60	S	Proceed STRAIGHT through a gully.
0.10	2.70	BR	Bear RIGHT onto a wide trail.
0.10	2.80	BL	Stay LEFT.
0.10	2.90	S	Go STRAIGHT through another gully.
0.10	3.00	T/L/R	Go through a challenging downhill obstacle course to a T-intersection. Turn LEFT, then a quick RIGHT.
0.20	3.20	BR	Trail bears RIGHT, back into the woods.
0.10	3.30	S	Enjoy a skateboarder-type route through a gully in the shape of a half-pipe.
0.20	3.40	T/L	Turn LEFT at the T-intersection and proceed up a hill.
0.20	3.60	BR	Bear to the RIGHT and up a hill.
0.10	3.70	L	Turn LEFT at the fork, into a pine forest.
0.10	3.80	BR	Bear RIGHT.
0.10	3.90	BL/T/L/L	Bear LEFT, then come to a T-intersection, turn LEFT again, proceed downhill and LEFT at the next fork.
0.30	4.20	BL	Bear LEFT.
0.10	4.30	BR	Bear RIGHT at fork.
0.20	4.50	S	Trail ends at sign.

🚲 NASSAU-SUFFOLK GREENBELT TRAIL

Trip Length:	18.00 miles
Difficulty:	Intermediate
Trail Configuration:	Out and Back
Elevation Change:	70 feet
Trail Type:	Singletrack

Pt. to Point	Cume	Turn	Landmark
0.00	0.00	S	Enter the trail at the back of the parking lot and continue STRAIGHT, past the Stillwell Woods Mountain Bike Trail sign. There will

Pt. to Point	Cume	Turn	Landmark
			be a large open field on the left.
0.40	0.40	BR/L	At the end of the field, bear RIGHT along the carriage trail, then quickly make the next LEFT onto singletrack marked with white blazes.
0.10	0.50	S	Proceed STRAIGHT over an intersecting trail.
0.10	0.60	L/L/R	Go LEFT down a steep hill then LEFT again at the bottom of the hill. Trail winds to the RIGHT down another slope.
0.10	0.70	BL	At the bottom of the slope, bear LEFT (away from the houses) and follow the trail that parallels the railroad tracks.
0.10	0.80	R/R	Turn RIGHT and proceed through a tunnel under the railroad tracks, and turn RIGHT on the other side.
0.10	0.90	L/L	Make the next LEFT up steep slope and follow the trail as it treacherously parallels the railroad tracks down below on the right. Trail continues up the hill to the LEFT, toward more manageable singletrack.
0.30	1.20	S	Cross over a road and enjoy some woodsy singletrack on the other side.
1.00	2.20	S	Come to a small parking lot on the north side of Jericho Turnpike. (Pathmark supermarket on right.) Cross over the road.
0.40	2.60	R	Cross over another road. Look for the continuation of the trail slightly to the RIGHT on the other side of the road.
0.50	3.10	S	Enjoy a nice singletrack climb.
0.80	3.90	S	Hiker section splits off from biker section. Stay on biker section.
0.10	4.00	L/L/S	Turn LEFT onto bridge over Northern State Parkway. After bridge, turn LEFT back onto trail, down a hill, then STRAIGHT over the parkway entrance ramp.
0.30	4.30	S	Come to the top of a hill.
0.10	4.40	R	Stay RIGHT at the fork.
0.30	4.70	BL	Bear LEFT at the fork.

Pt. to Point	Cume	Turn	Landmark
0.10	4.80	BL	Bear LEFT at the fork.
0.10	4.90	S	Proceed STRAIGHT over intersecting trail.
0.20	5.10	S	Proceed STRAIGHT through an underpass beneath the Long Island Expressway.
0.40	5.50	S	Cross over a road.
0.40	5.90	S	Cross an intersecting trail.
0.50	6.40	R/T/L/BR	Come to another road. Cross and proceed into a grassy area. Trail picks up on the RIGHT. At the T-intersection, turn LEFT, then bear RIGHT up a small slope.
0.40	6.80	R/L	Make a quick RIGHT then LEFT as trail begins to run parallel to a dead-end road.
0.20	7.00	S	Cross over Old Bethpage Road.
1.00	8.00	S	Cross another small road. The trail continues relatively flat through areas of low-lying vegetation.
0.20	8.20	S	Cross over an intersecting trail.
0.20	8.40	BL	Bear LEFT, continuing on the carriage trail.
0.10	8.50	S/BR/S	Continue STRAIGHT through a sandlot and take a path on the other side, bearing RIGHT. Continue STRAIGHT on wide, sandy trail.
0.30	8.80	BL	Bear LEFT at the fork.
0.10	8.90	R/L	Make a quick RIGHT, then LEFT.
0.10	9.00	S	Trail ends at Bethpage State Park parking lot. On right side of parking lot, a paved bike trail begins and continues south to Massapequa.

RIDES IN CONNECTICUT

19. HUNTINGTON STATE PARK

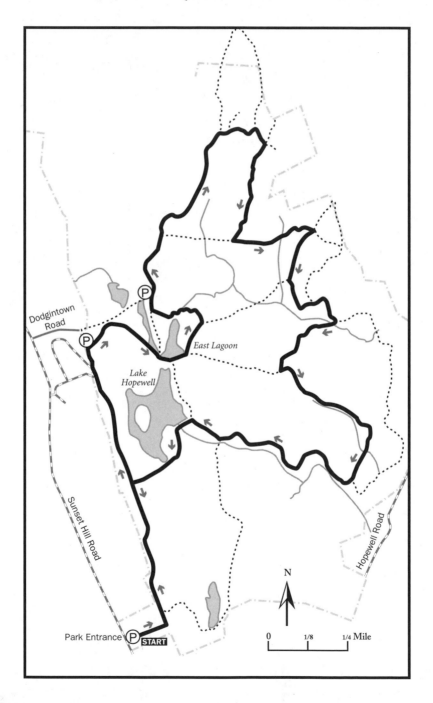

Dodgintown Road

East Lagoon

Lake Hopewell

Sunset Hill Road

Hopewell Road

N

Park Entrance · **START**

0   1/8   1/4 Mile

LOCATION:	Bethel, Connecticut
DISTANCE FROM NYC:	1.5 hours (60 miles)
TRAILS DESCRIBED:	Huntington Carriage Trail

Overview

Huntington is a large, sprawling park situated in a picturesque part of Connecticut amid rolling hills and horse farms. In fact, there is a working horse farm just north of the trailhead. The park offers numerous loops, including both wide, doubletrack trails and twisty singletrack trails. There are a number of lakes, ponds and creeks in the park which add to its allure. The view from the trailhead looks east, over the park, and offers a stunning panoramic landscape. Most of the trails are situated on a valley below the trailhead, with strenuous climbs from the valley to the surrounding ridges and hills. The park is dominated by mountain laurel, the state flower of Connecticut. Given its elevation (600-800 feet), the trails are often snow-covered in winter while other metro-area parks are clear; as a result, Huntington is a popular destination for cross-country skiers in winter.

Directions by Car

From the West Side (57th Street): Take the West Side Highway (9A) north, which becomes the Henry Hudson Parkway. After approximately 6 miles, exit onto 95 North (Cross Bronx Expressway). Continue on 95 North, which becomes the New England Thruway, for 38 miles to Exit 17, 33/136 Westport/Saugatuck. Travel on 136 North for 8.70 miles until Route 58. Turn left at the light onto 58 North. Continue on 58 North for 7 more miles. About 0.5 miles after the stop sign, turn right onto Sunset Hill Road. Continue on Sunset Hill Road for 0.7 miles. The park is on the right.

From the East Side: Take the FDR (62nd Street entrance used for mileage calculations) for 3 miles to the Willlis Avenue Bridge (Exit 18). Cross the bridge and follow the signs for 87 North (Deegan Expressway). Stay on 87 for 3 miles, then exit onto 95 North (Cross Bronx Expressway). Continue on 95 North, which becomes the New England Thruway, for 38 miles to Exit 17, 33/136 Westport/Saugatuck. Continue with West Side directions.

ᗣᗧ *HUNTINGTON CARRIAGE TRAIL*

Trip Length:	5.30 miles
Difficulty:	Intermediate/Advanced
Trail Configuration:	Loop
Elevation Change:	200 feet
Trail Type:	Carriage Trail; some Singletrack

Pt. to Point	Cume	Turn	Landmark
0.00	0.00	S	Start by going STRAIGHT, back from the parking lot and through the field, down the hill. Note the spectacular, panoramic views to the east as you plunge into the forest below.
0.10	0.10	T/L	At the bottom of the hill, turn LEFT at the T-junction.
0.50	0.60	S	Proceed STRAIGHT at the fork.
0.40	1.00	S	Continue on this wide, flat trail as it passes a horse farm on the left and then curves around to the right.
0.20	1.20	S	Pass a bridge on the left. Proceed STRAIGHT across the next bridge. Lake Hopewell is on the right, East Lagoon on the left.
0.10	1.30	T/L	At the T-intersection, turn LEFT, bordering on East Lagoon.
0.10	1.40	L	At the next intersection, turn LEFT. A dam at the northern end of the East Lagoon will be on your left as you cross over a small wooden bridge and head uphill.
0.20	1.60	S	Proceed down a steep descent with a creek on the right, a daunting rock formation to the left.
0.20	1.80	S	The trail flattens out.
0.10	1.90	L	Turn LEFT at the fork, up a rocky trail.
0.10	2.00	S	Notice a wide gully on the left and a boulder field in the distance.
0.10	2.10	S	At the end of the climb, go STRAIGHT,

Pt. to Point	Cume	Turn	Landmark
			crossing over an underground powerline right-of-way.
0.10	2.20	S	The trail curves around to the right; note a house on the left.
0.10	2.30	S	Proceed STRAIGHT, again over the powerline right-of-way.
0.10	2.40	L/L	Turn LEFT onto a singletrack into a cluster of pine trees for a quick break on a hilltop that offers seasonal views of the valley in the winter. Proceed back and turn LEFT back onto the trail.
0.10	2.50	S	The trail turns into a steep, technical descent.
0.20	2.70	BL	Bear to the LEFT as another trail merges in from the right.
0.10	2.80	S	Pass a singletrack trail on the right.
0.20	3.00	T/L	Turn LEFT at the T-intersection.
0.30	3.30	T/L	Turn LEFT at the T-intersection; note a road on the left as the trail heads up a slight grade.
0.40	3.70	T/L	Turn LEFT at the T-intersection.
0.20	3.90	S	The trail grade evens out onto a smooth, winding tail with a swamp on the left.
0.40	4.30	BR	Bear RIGHT at the fork with a bridge on the left.
0.10	4.40	L	At the next fork, turn LEFT and proceed across the dammed edge of Lake Hopewell and up the ensuing hill.
0.30	4.70	L	Turn LEFT back onto the trail that led into the park.
0.50	5.20	R	Turn RIGHT and proceed up the hill to the parking lot.
0.10	5.30	S	Back to the lot.

20. MIANUS RIVER PARK

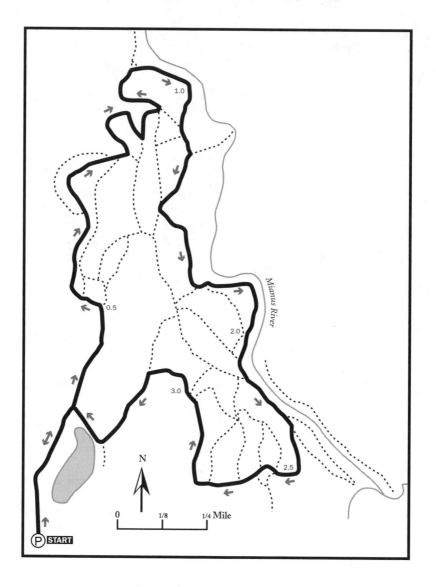

Mianus River

1.0

0.5

2.0

3.0

2.5

N

0   1/8   1/4 Mile

P START

LOCATION:	Greenwich, Connecticut
DISTANCE FROM NYC:	1 hour (35 miles)
TRAILS DESCRIBED:	Mianus River Loop

Overview

Mianus River Park is a small park on municipal land that is shared by the city of Stamford and the town of Greenwich. The two predominant trail types at Mianus are singletrack and carriage trails. Although the park is rather small, the many interconnecting trails make it very confusing, so be careful to follow the directions of the loop route described here. However, feel comfortable that even if you get lost, civilization is not far away.

Directions by Car

From the West Side (57th Street): Take the West Side Highway (9A) north, which becomes the Henry Hudson Parkway. After approximately 6 miles, exit onto 95 North (Cross Bronx Expressway). Continue on 95 North, which becomes the New England Thruway, for 25 miles until next 5 (Route 1-Riverside/Old Greenwich) in Connecticut. Follow the exit ramp over the freeway, and at the light turn left onto East Putnam Road (Route 1 South). At the third light (less than 1 mile), turn right onto River Road, and at the stop sign turn right onto Valley Road. Continue on Valley for 1 mile and turn left onto Cognewaugh. Continue on Cognewaugh for 2 miles to a parking lot on the right side. The lot comes soon after Shannon Lane.

From the East Side: Take the FDR (62nd Street entrance used for mileage calculations) for 3 miles to the Willlis Avenue Bridge (Exit 18). Cross the bridge and follow the signs for 87 North (Deegan Expressway). Stay on 87 for 3 miles, then exit onto 95 North (Cross Bronz Expressway). Continue on 95 North, which becomes the New England Thruway, for 24 miles until Exit 5. Continue with West Side directions.

Directions by Train

Take the Metro North New Haven Line to Riverside. Depart train and turn right out of the parking lot onto Oval Avenue. At the stop sign, turn right onto Riverside Avenue, which crosses over the railroad tracks.

Continue on Riverside for about half a mile and turn left at the light onto East Putnam Road. At the next light (less than half a mile), turn right onto River Road. Continue with driving directions.

ᚖ *MIANUS RIVER LOOP*

Trip Length:	3.70 miles
Difficulty:	Intermediate
Trail Configuration:	Loop
Elevation Change:	120 feet
Trail Type:	Singletrack

Pt. to Point	Cume	Turn	Landmark
0.00	0.00	S	Facing away from the road, the trailhead is on the back left side of the parking lot. The trail starts out as a relatively flat, wide carriage trail.
0.30	0.30	L	Trail forks. Make a LEFT onto a singletrack trail.
0.20	0.50	L	As the trail winds left over a stream, make another LEFT, up a steep hill, where you will probably have to walk your bike. Continue along this winding singletrack.
0.10	0.60	L	At a fork, go LEFT.
0.10	0.70	S	Notice a small trail to the right. Continue STRAIGHT, up a steep slope.
0.10	0.80	R	Another fork. Go RIGHT. Up ahead there is a trail coming in from the right, and a creek to your left.
0.20	1.00	S	Notice another trail coming in from the right, then pass over a small stream
0.05	1.05	BR	Another fork. Stay RIGHT.
0.05	1.10	T/L	The trail comes to a T-intersection. Turn LEFT.
0.10	1.20	R	Take a RIGHT turn down a gradual slope.
0.20	1.40	T/R	At the T-intersection turn RIGHT. This is near the boundary of the park and there are houses on the left.

Pt. to Point	Cume	Turn	Landmark
0.10	1.50	T/R	Trail ends at the T-intersection. Turn right onto the carriage trail.
0.20	1.70	L	Make a LEFT off the carriage trail onto a singletrack trail. This trail runs parallel to the river, which you will hear rushing by down below on the left. The trail is relatively flat at this point, but has low, tight underbrush and plenty of stumps and roots to slow you down.
0.20	1.90	BL	Notice a trail coming in from the left, and then a fork straight ahead. Bear LEFT onto the carriage trail. Stay on the main trail and ignore the spur trails to the left unless you want to take a break by the river.
0.10	2.00	S	Notice a path on the right. Stay STRAIGHT.
0.10	2.10	S	Notice another path on the right. Stay STRAIGHT.
0.20	2.30	S	Notice a triangular intersection and another carriage trail off to the right. Stay STRAIGHT.
0.10	2.40	R	Make a RIGHT onto a singletrack trail on the right.
0.10	2.50	R	After a nice climb, but not at the top of the hill, turn RIGHT onto another singletrack trail. If you see a "No Trespassing" sign, you have crossed the park boundary and gone too far; turn back.
0.20	2.70	S	The trail runs along a cliff that drops off precipitously to the right. Keep looking straight ahead!
0.10	2.80	R/L/R	Careful here: At the fork, make a RIGHT and then a quick LEFT at the next fork, then a quick RIGHT at the fork after that, going up a small slope.
0.10	2.90	S	Notice a spur trail to the left, which leads to a rocky overlook. Continue STRAIGHT, which goes down a steep hill.
0.10	3.00	T/R	At the T-intersection (with rocky slope on

Pt. to Point	Cume	Turn	Landmark
			the left), turn RIGHT.
0.05	3.05	T/L	At the next T-intersection, turn LEFT.
0.05	3.10	T/L	Turn LEFT at the next T-intersection onto a carriage trail.
0.20	3.30	S	Go around a group of boulders in the middle of the trail. Then notice a singletrack trail off to the left. Continue on the carriage trail as it winds around to the right.
0.10	3.40	T/L	At the T-intersection, make a LEFT. (The trail to the right is the first singletrack trail described at mile 0.3.) Stay on the carriage trail, which leads back to the parking lot.
0.30	3.70	S	You are back at the parking lot.

Maneuvering through a technical section in Huntington State Park

21. OLD MINE PARK

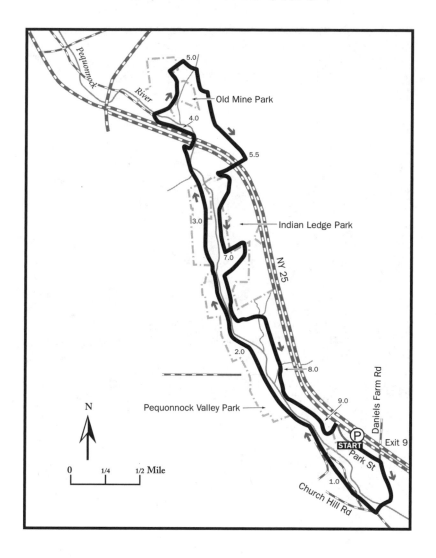

LOCATION:	Trumbull, Connecticut
DISTANCE FROM NYC:	1.5 hour (60 miles)
TRAILS DESCRIBED:	Old Mine Park Loop

Overview

Trumbull offers a unique combination of mountain-biking terrain that may appeal to both beginner and intermediate-level cyclists. The park is heavily wooded and includes three distinct sections: a rail-trail, a hilly loop, and technical singletrack. The unimproved rail-trail, once part of the Housotonic Railroad, is relatively flat and serves as a great warm-up for the more technical terrain later in the ride. Much of the trail is situated on a ledge overlooking the rushing Pequonnock River. At the end of the railroad bed section, the trail connects to Old Mine Park, named for a working mine that used to be situated there. The trails in Old Mine Park are steep, but not too technical. The final leg of the trail offers a few modest hills, but is notable for its tight turns and technical terrain over frequently appearing root and boulder fields. In addition, there are multiple water crossings in this section, especially when the trail traverses an abandoned reservoir. For a shorter route, cross the river prior to reaching Old Mine Park, as indicated in mileage marker 3.2.

Directions by Car

From the West Side (57th Street): Take the West Side Highway (9A) north, which becomes the Henry Hudson Parkway. After approximately 6 miles, exit onto 95 North (Cross Bronx Expressway). Continue on 95 North, which becomes the New England Thruway, for 48 miles to Exit 27A, "CT25 CT8 Trumbull/Waterbury." Follow 25/8 North for 3.7 miles, where the highway forks. Bear left and continue with 25 North. Continue 2.5 miles to Exit 9, Daniels Farm Road. At the stop sign, turn left onto Daniels Farm Road, toward Trumbull. After crossing over the highway, make the first right onto Park Street (note a sign for 25 South) and make a second left into a commuter parking lot. There are two trail heads to Old Mine Park. This is where the ride will finish.

From the East Side: Take the FDR (62nd Street entrance used for mileage calculations) for 3 miles to the Willlis Avenue Bridge (Exit 18). Cross the bridge and follow the signs for 87 North (Deegan Expressway). Stay on

87 for 3 miles, then exit onto 95 North (Cross Bronx Expressway). Continue on 95 North, which becomes the New England Thruway, for 48 miles to Exit 27A, "CT25 CT8 Trumbull/Waterbury." Continue with West Side directions.

🚲 OLD MINE PARK

Trip Length:	9.40 miles
Difficulty:	Intermediate
Trail Configuration:	Loop
Elevation Change:	300 feet
Trail Type:	Unimproved Rail-Trail; Singletrack

Pt. to Point	Cume	Turn	Landmark
0.00	0.00	R	Head out of the parking lot and turn RIGHT onto Daniels Farm Road.
0.60	0.60	R	At the light at the bottom of the hill, turn RIGHT onto Church Hill Road.
0.10	0.70	R	Turn RIGHT onto Tait Road.
0.10	0.80	S	The trailhead is on the left, as Tait Road bends to the right. While wide and flat, like most rail-trails, this one is somewhat rocky and has its share of bumps.
0.30	1.10	S	Pass over a small creek. There are a number of streams and small waterfalls coming down the hill from the left and emptying into the river on the right. The park is heavily wooded and you can hear the loud rush of the Pequonnock River on the left.
0.70	1.80	S	Continue STRAIGHT past a spur trail on the right.
0.40	2.20	S	Note a trail on the right that leads down to a bridge over the river.
0.70	2.90	S	Continue STRAIGHT past another spur trail on the right.
0.30	3.20	S	Continue STRAIGHT past a singletrack trail on the right. (*Note:* For a shorter route, turn right here and proceed to mile

Pt. to Point	Cume	Turn	Landmark
			6.3 in these directions.)
0.30	3.50	S	Cross over a road, Whitney Avenue. Note sign for Parlor Rock Park.
0.30	3.80	R	Before the trail ends at the Merritt Parkway, make a hard RIGHT up a short, steep slope onto a singletrack trail.
0.20	4.00	L	Follow the singletrack underneath a double bridge (note a creek on the right) then LEFT at fork up a rocky slope toward a road. Travel underneath an expressway sign.
0.10	4.10	R	Follow trail to the RIGHT into the woods, where the trail becomes rocky and technical, and runs alongside a fence on the left.
0.20	4.30	R	Trail leads into Old Mine Park. Pass a small building on the right, then turn RIGHT over a short bridge directly behind the building.
0.10	4.40	BR	Bear RIGHT as the trail forks.
0.10	4.50	S	Slope of the trail becomes steep.
0.20	4.70	BR	Near the top of the hill, bear RIGHT at the fork, continuing on singletrack.
0.10	4.80	R	Cross a small stream. The trail heads up to a road. Turn RIGHT on the road.
0.10	4.90	R	Turn RIGHT again onto Skating Pond Road.
0.20	5.10	R	Turn RIGHT onto Teller Road. The elevation is high enough to see the Long Island Sound in the distance, before the road takes you downhill.
0.50	5.60	R	Turn RIGHT onto Whitney Avenue.
0.30	5.90	L	Travel under a bridge, then make the next LEFT into Indian Ledge Park.
0.10	6.00	R/L/R	The trail begins again inside a guardrail on the right. Inside the guardrail, turn RIGHT, traveling downhill to a footbridge. Turn LEFT over the bridge then make a quick RIGHT.
0.10	6.10	S	The trail passes a small park on the left. Continue on flat but rocky singletrack into a pine forest.

Pt. to Point	Cume	Turn	Landmark
0.20	6.30	S	Pass a singletrack trail on the right (this connects with the rail-trail on the other side of the river).
0.40	6.70	BL	At the fork, stay LEFT.
0.10	6.80	S	Cross a stream.
0.10	6.90	BL	Stay LEFT at the fork.
0.10	7.00	S	When a fallen tree appears at an approximately 30-degree angle to the trail on the left, use the tree as a guide to a singletrack trail up the hillside on the left.
0.20	7.20	R	Turn RIGHT at the top of the hill and head through a lush canopy of mountain laurel.
0.10	7.30	T/R	Turn RIGHT at the T-intersection and carefully descend down a steep, tight singletrack.
0.10	7.40	L	Turn LEFT, back onto the wide trail along the river, following the white blazes.
0.10	7.50	R	Stay RIGHT, bearing toward the river as the trail becomes more technical, with a number of roots and rocks. This section ends at a rock formation jutting into the river, providing an impressive view downstream.
0.20	7.70	BL	Bear LEFT (away from the river) and climb up a short hill.
0.10	7.80	S	Follow the trail down a steep slope, into a field that used to be a reservoir.
0.10	7.90	BR	Follow the wide trail through the field, bearing RIGHT at two consecutive forks.
0.20	8.10	L	Turn LEFT at the next fork and proceed through a creek; prepare to get wet!
0.20	8.30	S	Go through another small water crossing.
0.10	8.40	BR	Cross another creek and bear RIGHT on the other side.
0.10	8.50	S	Cross an intersecting trail.
0.10	8.60	S/L/R	Continue STRAIGHT up a hill, turn LEFT at the top, then RIGHT down a slope. Walk your bike through a small field of large boulders.

Pt. to Point	Cume	Turn	Landmark
0.10	8.70	S	Be careful as the trail becomes quite steep and rocky, leading to a gradual climb with the river on the right, and steep rock formations on the left.
0.20	8.90	BL	Bear LEFT at the fork at the top of a hill; then enjoy the ensuing descent.
0.10	9.00	S	Practice your jumping through a number of drop-offs.
0.10	9.10	BL	At the bottom of the hill, bear LEFT at the fork.
0.10	9.20	L/R	Travel down a slope and LEFT across a creek. Turn RIGHT and exit the forest.
0.20	9.40	R	Turn RIGHT into the parking lot.

A typical drop in Connecticut.

RIDES IN
NEW JERSEY

New Jersey rides from *RIDE GUIDE: New Jersey Mountain Biking*, Third Edition, by Joshua M. Pierce. ISBN: 978-0-933855-25-0

22. ALLAIRE STATE PARK

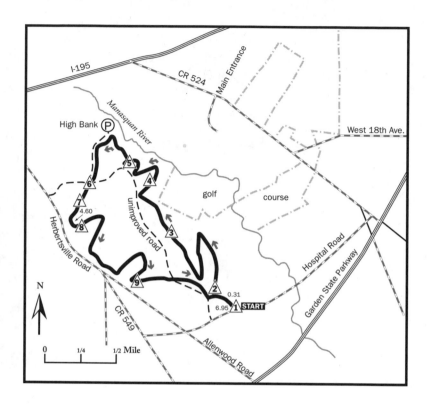

4.41 miles
Farmingdale, Monmouth Co.

HIGHLIGHTS	Easy – Moderate
TERRAIN:	Very sandy, some roots, logs
TOPOGRAPHY:	Many short hills, several longer ones
DIFFICULTY:	Easy to moderately difficult
TRAIL TYPES:	Mainly singletrack, some wider trails and fire roads

GENERAL INFORMATION
Allaire State Park is a part of the New Jersey State Park Service. For more information, contact:

Allaire State Park
PO Box 220
Farmingdale, NJ 07727
(732) 938-2371
www.state.nj.us/dep/parksandforests/parks/allaire.html

Directions: These directions are not for the main entrance to Allaire State Park. They are for the multi-use trail parking lot on Hospital Road. There is no mountain biking from the main entrance, and if you do wind up there, you will be directed by a park ranger to the Hospital Road parking lot.

From the Garden State Parkway southbound: Take Exit 98. Follow signs for Route 34 South. Once on 34 take a right at the first light onto Allenwood Road. At the T-intersection, turn right onto Atlantic Avenue. Then turn left at the first intersection onto Hospital Road. The parking lot is half a mile on the right.

From Interstate 195: Use Exit 31A toward Lakewood. Take a left onto Herbertsville Road at the first intersection. Bear left onto Allenwood Road. Turn left onto Hospital Road. The parking lot is half a mile on the left.

Size: About 9 miles of trails on a total of 3,086 acres.

Park Hours: Trails open dawn to dusk, year-round.

Entry Fee: There is no fee to use the multi-use trail located off of the Hospital Road parking lot. If you do enter the main gate to visit the historic Allaire Village, the entrance fee is $2 on weekdays and $3 on weekends and holidays from Memorial Day through Labor Day.

Trail Classifications: There are no difficulty ratings for the trails at Allaire. Overall, I would consider the trails to be moderate in difficulty.

Trail Maps: Trail maps are available at the gate at the main entrance to the park.

Restrooms: There are no facilities by the multi-use trail area.

Closest Mountain Biking Area: Manasquan Reservoir is less than 5 miles west of Allaire in Howell. Hartshorne and Huber Woods are about 15 miles north.

Other Park Activities: Hiking, horseback riding, canoeing, fishing, hunting, camping, and sightseeing.

OVERVIEW

Allaire State Park is predominantly an historical site around which camping, hiking, and biking facilities have grown through numerous acquisitions of land under the Green Acres Program.

History: Allaire began as an iron forgery in the early 1790s. In 1822, the property was purchased by James P. Allaire, who turned the furnace into a self-contained community of up to 500 people, where he produced castings and pig iron for building steamship engines and boilers. The village declined in the 1840s, but the village was preserved by Arthur Brisbane, who purchased the property in 1907. In 1941, the property was deeded to the state of New Jersey and has subsequently tripled in size over the past 50 years.

Terrain/Trail Composition: The terrain at Allaire consists of rolling hills and sandy soil. Depending upon the weather and how much rainfall has recently accumulated, the soil can be extremely sandy and difficult to ride. In places it can be like attempting to ride on the beach at the ocean. If the weather has not been too arid, the trail should be fairly hardpacked except in a few spots. The sandy soil tends to become rutted out easily where a large volume of people have used the singletrack trail, especially on the steeper sections. There are numerous small log obstacles, but relatively few large obstacles at all on the trail. There is a noticeable lack of rocks at Allaire in general.

SPECIFIC TRAIL DIRECTIONS

Intermediate Loop: There are three marked trails in this section of Allaire, and a maze of unmarked ones. The route described below follows the orange trail in general and converges with both the white and blue trails at different points. The trail is well marked with plastic marker posts, which were new and in great condition in the autumn of 2004.

There are a plethora of interconnecting trails and dead-end spurs crisscrossing the marked trail. Once you become familiar with this trail, you can use these extraneous trails to link up your favorite sections of the marked trail, or to create new or multiple loop combinations within the multi-use trail area. The printed map at the information board at the trailhead does not mention any of the trail markings and should not be used to try to follow the trail, but the actual trail is marked well enough that you should be able to follow it without getting lost. There are more than 40 intersections detailed in the route below. At times, it could get very confusing and frustrating trying to follow the written directions at every intersection. In these situations, it is probably easier to follow the posted arrows unless you get to an intersection that is poorly marked.

Total route distance: 4.41 miles
Ride time for an *intermediate* rider: 0.5–1.0 hours

GPS Waypoints and Elevation in feet:

GPS 1	N40 08.448 W74 07.355	115'
GPS 2	N40 08.464 W74 07.425	105'
GPS 3	N40 08.813 W74 07.977	120'
GPS 4	N40 09.067 W74 08.406	155'
GPS 5	N40 09.210 W74 08.433	95'
GPS 6	N40 09.026 W74 08.697	95'
GPS 7	N40 08.922 W74 08.799	110'
GPS 8	N40 08.769 W74 08.726	135'
GPS 9	N40 08.331 W74 07.978	145'

Pt. to Point	Cume	Turn	Landmark
0.00 GPS 1	0.00 115'	S	From the west end of the **Hospital Road** parking lot, there is an information board with a trailhead next to it.
0.04 GPS 2	0.04 105'	S	Across **fire road** onto **singletrack**. Trail is marked orange.
0.01	0.05	R	Onto tiny **singletrack** to take the **Orange Trail** in the recommended **counter-clockwise** direction.
0.27	0.31	S	Across old, overgrown paved road.
0.02	0.33	S	Through intersection.
0.37	0.70	L	At **three-way intersection**. Follow signs for **Orange** and **White Trails**. Trail is flat and sandy.
0.20 GPS 3	0.90 120'	R	Onto more primitive singletrack trail.
0.26	1.16	BR	Onto wider trail.
0.09	1.25	S	At **four-way intersection** at the bottom of a short hill. Stay on **Orange Trail** where the White Trail turns left. Head up a steep, gravelly hill.
0.23	1.48	L	To follow the **Orange Trail** at the second intersection.
0.08	1.56	S	Stay on the **Orange Trail**.
0.06	1.62	BR	Stay on the **Orange Trail**. Cross clearing with fencing blocking off an old trail. Follow the most distinct trail and Orange signs through a maze-like area.
0.08 GPS 4	1.70 155'	R	Onto a singletrack trail heading into deeper woods. The trail is level for a short bit, then switches back to the **left** and navigates down a long, twisty **downhill**.
0.17	1.87	L	At sign to head downhill again.
0.07 GPS 5	1.94 95'	L	At fork to stay on **Orange Trail.**
0.04	1.98	L	Toward deeper woods to stay on **Orange.**
0.39 GPS 6	2.37 95'	S	Across wide, very sandy trail. Follow **Orange.**
0.03	2.40	S	Stay on wide trail. Starts to head uphill and becomes **extremely sandy** (hint: singletrack trail that runs parallel to sand pit is easier to

Pt. to Point	Cume	Turn	Landmark
			ride, but trail becomes steep and the sand is impossible to ride).
0.15 GPS 7	2.55 160'	L	Trail emerges into clearing by power lines at top of hill. Turn **left** to get on singletrack hugging edge of clearing. Then enter white pine forest.
0.08	2.63	S	At end of sandy oval back into the woods on the **Orange Trail.**
0.05	2.68	R	Onto **Orange** and **Blue** singletrack.
0.12 GPS 8	2.80 135'	S	Stay on **Orange Trail** (Blue Trail turns left).
0.09	2.89	L	At four-way intersection as trail nears Herbertsville Road. Trail then runs roughly parallel to road.
0.25	3.14	S	Stay on **Orange Trail** at four-way intersection (**Blue Trail** rejoins orange).
0.16	3.30	BR	Stay on **Orange Trail** (Blue Trail diverges to left).
0.05	3.35	S	At four-way intersection. Stay on **Orange Trail.**
0.10	3.40	BR	Up tiny hill to stay on **Orange Trail.**
0.23	3.63	S	Go **straight** down steep little hill. Then continue straight past numerous diverging trails and head up hill at the other end.
0.09 GPS 9	3.72 145'	T/L	At T-intersection onto flat trail.
0.02	3.74	BR	At first fork onto narrower singletrack trail. Stay on **Orange** (trail traverses a small clearing and becomes sandy).
0.17	3.91	R	At fork to stay on the **Orange Trail.** Head into woods.
0.08	3.99	L	Onto singletrack, then take first **right** to stay on **Orange Trail.** Follow signs. Trail takes on different characteristics as it enters a hardwood forest. Trail becomes tighter
0.37	4.36	BR	To head back to car (left starts the loop over again).
0.01 GPS 2	4.37 105'	S	Recross gravel road.
0.04 GPS 1	4.41 115'		Back to parking lot. End of route.

23. CHEESEQUAKE STATE PARK

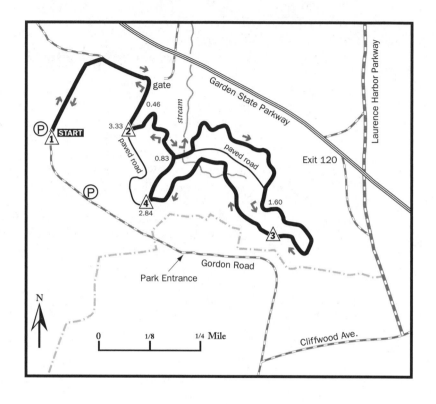

3.37 miles
Matawan, Middlesex Co.

HIGHLIGHTS	**Moderate**
TERRAIN:	**Some roots, multiple log crossings**
TOPOGRAPHY:	**Roller-coaster-esque, with a few longer hills**
DIFFICULTY:	**Intermediate**
TRAIL TYPES:	**Mostly singletrack, with some connecting fire road**

GENERAL INFORMATION

Cheesequake State Park is a part of the New Jersey Division of Parks and Forestry. For more information, contact:

Cheesequake State Park
300 Gordon Road
Matawan, NJ 07747
(732) 566-2161
www.state.nj.us/dep/parksandforests/parks/cheesequake.html

Directions: From the Garden State Parkway: Take Exit 120 onto southbound Laurence Harbor Parkway. Turn right onto Cliffwood Avenue at the first light. Turn right onto Gordon Road at the next light and follow it into the park. After going through the tollbooth, continue straight and park in the first parking lot on the left.

From Route 34 South: Turn left onto Disbrow Road at the light just south of the Marketplace Shopping Plaza. Take a right at the end of Disbrow. Turn left at the first light onto Gordon Road and follow it into the park. After going through the tollbooth, continue straight and park in the first parking lot on the left.

Size: 15 to 20 miles of trails on 1,361 acres. However, bikes are allowed only on the multi-use trail, which is about 3 miles long.

Park Hours: 8 a.m. to 6 p.m., open until 8 p.m. between Memorial Day and Labor Day.

Entry Fee: $5 per car weekdays, $10 per car weekends (only between

Memorial Day and Labor Day). There is no fee to walk or ride a bike into the park. A New Jersey State Park Pass costs $35 and is good for a year. It gives you unlimited access to any of the state parks (Cheesequake, Allaire, Round Valley, Sandy Hook).

Trail Classification: The trail is not marked for difficulty. I consider it an intermediate trail.

Trail Maps: Trail maps are available at the ranger station by the tollbooth.

Restrooms: There are seasonal restrooms in the ranger station by the tollbooth.

Nearby Mountain Biking Areas: The Henry Hudson Trail is about 5 miles east of Cheesequake. Hartshorne Woods Park is about 15 miles east.

Other Park Activities: Hiking, picnicking, camping, softball, fishing, and swimming in the Hooks Creek Lake are all popular at Cheesequake. Also, sledding, ice skating, and cross-country skiing are popular during the winter months.

OVERVIEW
The trails at Cheesequake contain some great terrain for mountain biking. Unfortunately, the great majority is off limits to mountain bikes. There are a lot of interesting sites and activities at Cheesequake, which is geared heavily toward education and family fun. Mountain biking is an afterthought at best.

Terrain/Trail Composition: The terrain at Cheesequake is relatively technical. The trails are almost entirely singletrack, connected with paved roads. There are many log pile crossings on the singletrack sections, mostly rideable. The terrain is very roller-coaster-esque and challenging. There is some great riding at Cheesequake. Unfortunately, the majority of the park is accessible only on foot.

History: Cheesequake officially opened in June of 1940. The earliest known inhabitants of the area were the Lenni Lenape Indians. Evidence of their existence dates back some 5,000 years.

SPECIFIC TRAIL DIRECTIONS

Intermediate Loop: The described route is the only trail at Cheesequake where it is legal to ride a mountain bike. There are many miles of other trails at Cheesequake, but bikes are off limits on all of them. Out of about 15 to 20 trail miles, this 3.5-mile loop encompasses all of the rideable sections of the park.

The route is marked with round white signs. There are several points where sections of the loop come pretty close to one another, so be careful not to get on an incorrect trail section.

Total route distance: 3.37 miles
Ride time for an *intermediate* rider: 0.5–1.0 hours

GPS Waypoints and Elevation Heights:

GPS 1	N40 26.166 W74 15.925	65'
GPS 2	N40 26.175 W74 15.706	60'
GPS 3	N40 25.970 W74 15.296	90'
GPS 4	N40 26.075 W74 15.693	90'

Pt. to Point	Cume	Turn	Landmark
0.00	0.00	L	Onto paved road traveling away from park
GPS 1	65'		entrance. Take it down to end.
0.21	0.21	R	At stop sign.
0.11	0.32	R	At next intersection. Go around gate.
0.16	0.48	L	Onto beginning of **Multi-Use Trail**
GPS 2	60'		singletrack. Trail heads gradually downhill, then up and down small hills. Trail is a mix of sandy dirt with roots and log crossings (which can be extremely slippery when wet).
0.35	0.83	L	Onto paved road.
0.09	0.92	L	Onto singletrack Multi-Use Trail.
0.18	1.10		Short, steep climb.
0.22	1.32		Longer, more gradual climb.
0.07	1.39	BR	Just before clearing to stay on **White Circle Trail**. Trail has a few downs and ups before climbing up to a ridge above the Garden State Parkway.
0.35	1.74	L	Onto gravel road.

Pt. to Point	Cume	Turn	Landmark
GPS 3	90'		
0.03	1.77	L	First left onto singletrack trail, bear left immediately.
0.13	1.90	S	Cross dirt road. Continue on **White Trail** singletrack straight ahead. This next section is rooty.
0.07	1.97	S	Cross a small wooden bridge.
0.23	2.20	S	Cross a small wooden bridge at the bottom of a technical little downhill.
0.21	2.41	L	Trail turns left at the bottom of a hill and crosses a small wooden bridge.
0.04	2.45	S	Singletrack trail heads up a big, steep, technical hill.
0.09	2.54		Top of hill. Trail levels out.
0.10	2.64	R	Onto paved road. Start heading downhill.
GPS 4	90'		
0.12	2.76	L	Off paved road onto **White Trail** singletrack before the bottom of the hill.
0.20	2.96		**Short, technical climb.**
0.17	3.11	R	Onto paved road.
GPS 2	60'		
0.13	3.23	T/L	At T-intersection.
0.11	3.34	L	At intersection.
0.03	3.37		Back to parking lot. End of route.

Photo by Joshua M. Pierce

Getting traction on a rocky climb.

24. HARTSHORNE WOODS PARK

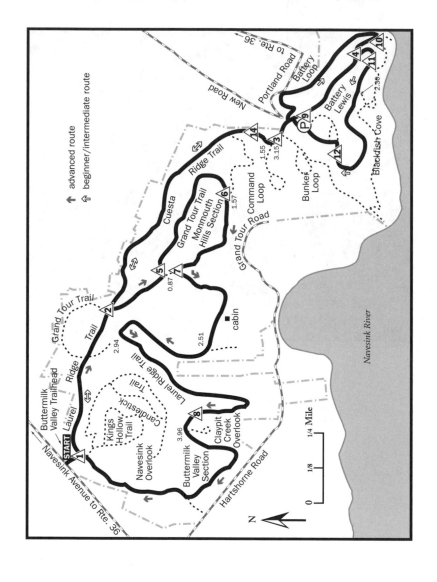

4.76, 4.91, 2.87 miles
Middletown, Monmouth Co.

HIGHLIGHTS	Beginner – Advanced
TERRAIN:	Sandy, some roots, logs
TOPOGRAPHY:	Roller-coaster-esque, several longer climbs
DIFFICULTY:	Hybrid-friendly to difficult
TRAIL TYPES:	Mainly singletrack, some fire road

GENERAL INFORMATION
Hartshorne Woods Park is a part of the Monmouth County Park System. For more information, contact:

Monmouth County Park System
805 Newman Springs Road
Lincroft, NJ 07738
(908) 842-4000
www.monmouthcountyparks.com
info@monmouthcountyparks.com

Directions: Hartshorne Woods Park is located off of Route 36 in the hills that make up one of the highest points directly on the Eastern seaboard of the United States. The park is less than 5 miles from the Atlantic Ocean in Middletown. It can be reached by taking Exit 117 off the Garden State Parkway or taking Route 35 to Route 36. Take Route 36 east 12 miles from the Parkway and follow the following directions to one of the two parking areas at Hartshorne.

Buttermilk Valley Parking Area: Take the Scenic Drive Exit. Turn right at the stop sign at the end of the off-ramp onto Navesink Avenue. The parking lot is less than half a mile on the left.

Rocky Point Parking Area: Continue on Route 36 past the Scenic Drive Exit. Follow highway downhill toward Sandy Hook. Turn right near the bottom of the hill onto Portland Road and follow the road up a long hill. Turn left onto New Road and follow it into the park. The parking lot is straight ahead.

Size: 15 miles of trails on 736 acres.

Park Hours: 8 a.m. to dusk, year-round.

Entry Fee: No charge.

Trail Classifications: All trails are marked by a symbol designating its accessibility and the skill level needed for completing the trail. All the trails in all the Monmouth County Park System share this trail rating system.

Note: The trail rating system is designed for hiking and is not as accurate for biking.

Green Circles indicate highly maintained gradual grade trails designed primarily for walking.

Blue Squares signify multiple-use trails with moderate grades and relatively easy access.

Black Diamonds indicate steep grades, challenging terrain and minimal maintenance on trails designed for experienced bikers, hikers, and equestrians.

Trail Maps: There is a large trail map and information board in the dismount area by the parking lot. Trail maps are available there to take along.

Restrooms: There is a portable toilet by the Buttermilk Valley trailhead and another one halfway around the Grand Tour Trail.

Closest Mountain Biking Area: Huber Woods Park is only a few miles southwest in Locust. The eastern end of the Henry Hudson Trail is about 3 miles west of Hartshorne off Route 36.

Other Park Activities: Hiking, horseback riding, and trail running are all popular activities at Hartshorne. All trails except the Candlestick Trail and the King's Hollow Trail, which are off limits to bikes, are multi-use trails and are shared by all users. It is also possible to cross-country ski and fish at Hartshorne. Group cabin camping is available by reservation.

OVERVIEW

Hartshorne is one of the most popular and heavily trafficked mountain biking areas in New Jersey. A fun place to ride located on a hill overlooking Sandy Hook and New York City, Hartshorne has something for just about everyone. As a result, it tends to get very crowded at Hartshorne on the weekends.

History: Hartshorne Woods Park's original owner was Richard Hartshorne, who first visited the area in 1670. In the early 1990s, the trails at Hartshorne were completely different than they are today. The trails were based around the Navesink Overlook (Candlestick Trail), which served as a hub for the multitude of trails that stemmed off it. In 1993, many of the existing trails that had become very rutted out due to overuse were permanently closed off while the entire system of trails that exists today were cut and opened to public use.

Dismount Area: There is a strip of wide fire road about 50 yards long just off the Buttermilk Valley trailhead and parking lot that is visibly posted from every direction with signs that read "Dismount Area." There is only one parking lot for Hartshorne Woods Park, and almost all the people using the area start and finish here. As a result, this is the most heavily congested area in the park. As a bicyclist, you are required to dismount and walk your bike through this section of trail. If courtesy and goodwill toward others are not incentive enough for you to follow the rules, park rangers routinely wait at the bottom of the hill in this section and hand out tickets to anyone who tries to ride through the area.

Candlestick Trail/King's Hollow Trail: These trails were made off limits to bikes during the 1995 season and are designated as hiking trails only. Getting caught on your bike in this area will also result in a ticket.

Terrain/Trail Composition: Overall, the terrain at Hartshorne Woods is fast and dry in comparison to other New Jersey areas. The ground is very smooth, and there is a noticeable lack of exposed rock. The soil is somewhat on the sandy side, but given its location—less than 5 miles from Sandy Hook—it is not nearly as sandy as you would expect. There are a few drawn-out hills at Hartshorne, but as a rule the hills are fairly short, yet ferocious. The woods in this area are dense and surprisingly lush and deep green. Other than in the midst of a long dry spell or drought, the sandy surface reverts into a fine, smooth dirt, which mountain bike tires stick well to, but which is still very fast.

Within Hartshorne Woods there are any number of combinations of trails to ride. Hartshorne Woods Park itself uses a system for rating the difficulty of their trails that borrows the symbols from the world of alpine skiing. Candlestick and Kings Hollow Trails are designated easy walking trails and are demarcated by a circle. Laurel Ridge and Cuesta Ridge Trails are designated moderate and marked with a square. The Grand Tour Trail is designated challenging, for serious biking and hiking and is marked with a diamond. In reality though, these designations do not really apply once you get on a bike. The Candlestick Trail, when it used to be legal, could be as challenging as any trail at Hartshorne, despite its designation as an easy trail. Everything from speed to direction of travel on any given trail can change the feel or even the difficulty of the ride. Though this is something that is generally true at most mountain biking areas, it is one of the very keys to riding at Hartshorne. While the Laurel Ridge Trail may have a gradual uphill culminating in a mad rushing downhill in the clockwise direction, climbing the same hill in the counterclockwise direction is a much more difficult endeavor. Combining different sections of various trails with directional travel creates a seemingly endless number of different rides. My advice when riding Hartshorne is to explore as many trails as you can. Since the geographical size of the park is fairly small (736 acres), it is very hard to get lost for too long.

SPECIFIC TRAIL DIRECTIONS
Beginner/Intermediate Ride: This route starts from the Buttermilk Valley Parking Area. It consists entirely of primitive, unpaved fire road and paved road. The overall structure is a 1.5-mile spur out to a 1.5-mile loop and back down the 1.5-mile spur to the parking lot. The spur climbs about 150 feet from the parking lot out to the paved loop, so think about the fun downhill heading back to the car while you are climbing at the beginning. The unpaved fire road portion of this route can be ridden without the paved section if you are looking for a shorter route. If at any point along the first 1.5 miles you feel as though you have gotten in over your head, turn around and head back down to the parking lot.

Total route distance: 4.76 miles
Ride time for a *recreational* rider: 1.0–2.0 hours

GPS Waypoints and Elevation Heights:

GPS 1	N40 24.066 W74 00.747	50'	
GPS 2	N40 23.994 W74 00.107	215'	
GPS 3	N40 23.525 W73 59.398	225'	
GPS 4	N40 23.226 W73 59.022	120'	
GPS 3	N40 23.525 W73 59.398	225'	
GPS 2	N40 23.994 W74 00.107	215'	
GPS 1	N40 24.066 W74 00.747	50'	

Pt. to Point	Cume	Turn	Landmark
GPS 1	50'		From the parking lot walk your bike into the **dismount area** and turn left onto the **Laurel Ridge Trail**. Walk your bike part way up the first incline before beginning to ride.
0.00	0.00	S	Climb up the **Laurel Ridge Trail**. This trail is a fire road. The hills are fairly steep and long, and do not fight, because there is plenty of loose gravel on the climbs for everyone.
0.12	0.12	S	Up the loose gravel hill.
0.08	0.20	BL	After the trail levels out it bears left and goes downhill for a short while.
0.30	0.50	S	Start to climb up a long hill.
0.10	0.60	S	Top of hill. Go straight at the intersection.
GPS 2	215'		The fire road is relatively level with only small hills. At this intersection the **Laurel Ridge Trail** ends and the **Cuesta Ridge Trail** begins.
0.77	1.37	S	Pass a right turn for the **Grand Tour Trail**
0.05	1.42	BR	Take the right fork to stay on the **Cuesta Ridge Trail**.
0.13	1.55	L	Onto paved road (**Battery Loop**). If you feel you have gotten in over your head, you can turn around at any point and head back down to the parking lot. From here the route makes a loop on a hilly paved road back to this point before returning to the Buttermilk Valley parking area the way you came.
GPS 3	225'		
0.10	1.65	BL	At five-way intersection. Pass one gate, cross

Pt. to Point	Cume	Turn	Landmark
			another intersection and pass a second gate following signs for **Battery Loop**.
0.41	2.06	S	At intersection. **Rocky Point** to the left goes
GPS 4	120'		to an overlook of the **Navesink River**.
0.14	2.20	S	At intersection.
0.05	2.25	BL	At the **steep grade** sign. Paved road goes down steep hill.
0.05	2.30	S	Stay on **Battery Loop**. Left turn is for **Blackfish Cove**, which will take you all the way down to a pier on the **Navesink River**.
0.15	2.45	S	Start long, steep climb.
0.37	2.82	BL	Pass Battery Lewis.
0.15	2.97	S	Stay on paved road.
0.06	3.03	L	Go past two gates and head back up to **Cuesta Ridge Trail**.
0.12	3.15	R	Back onto **Cuesta Ridge Trail**. Follow it
GPS 3	225'		straight all the way back to parking lot.
0.96	4.11	S	At intersection. Trail goes down *long fast*
GPS 2	215'		*hill.*
0.19	4.30	S	At bottom of hill.
0.10	4.40	BL	Trail turns left and goes up one last short climb before going downhill back to parking lot.
0.31	4.71	S	Get off bike at **dismount area**.
0.02	4.73	R	In the heart of the **dismount area**.
0.03	4.76		Back to parking lot. End of route.
GPS 1	50'		

Advanced Loop: This loop starts from the Buttermilk Valley Parking Area. There are a number of popular advanced loops to be ridden at Hartshorne as the trails exist today. One of the most popular, and certainly one of my favorites, is described below. This loop is an advanced trail, and the majority of it is singletrack.

This route covers all the geographical regions of the park and approximately 5 of the 11 trail-miles, but it is by no means the only option in the park. My advice is to explore as many trails as you can. Several of my favorite sections of trail at Hartshorne are not on this loop.

Total route distance: 4.91 miles
Ride time for an *advanced* rider: 0.5–1.0 hours

GPS Waypoints and Elevation Heights:

GPS 1	N40 24.066 W74 00.747	50'
GPS 2	N40 23.994 W74 00.107	215'
GPS 5	N40 23.816 W73 59.964	80'
GPS 6	N40 23.633 W73 59.636	60'
GPS 7	N40 23.811 W73 59.957	55'
GPS 8	N40 23.567 W74 00.544	180'

Pt. to Point	Cume	Turn	Landmark
GPS 1	25'		From the parking lot walk your bike into the **dismount area** and turn left onto the **Laurel Ridge Trail**. Walk your bike part way up the first incline before beginning to ride.
0.00	0.00	S	Follow the fire road up, down, and around. This series of hills is not very technical, but it usually seems to be the most painful part of this ride. I always feel like I am riding in slow motion, no matter how hard I push.
0.60 GPS 2	0.60 215'	R	At the **top** of the second hill turn right onto the **Grand Tour Trail**. This trail is almost entirely **singletrack**. This is where the fun begins. After the first few turns, the trail widens out and dips downhill.
0.27 GPS 5	0.87 80'	L	Near the bottom of the steep, banked downhill take the left turn. This left fork levels out and becomes singletrack again. There are many log obstacles to cross in this section, and it is very roller-coaster-esque.
0.70 GPS 6	1.57 60'	S	Continue straight when a trail comes in from the left. This section contains a number of off-camber log crossings.
0.21	1.78	R	Onto a wider, sandy trail.
0.26 GPS 7	2.04 55'	L	Stay on the **Grand Tour Trail**, which becomes singletrack again. **Do not** follow the **trailhead** sign. Eventually you will pass a **cabin** on the left (which may be obscured

Pt. to Point	Cume	Turn	Landmark
			by foliage). Stay to the right.
0.47	2.51	**T/R**	At the T where the singletrack dumps out onto a multitrack trail. You will pass another set of chopped trees and eventually come to a **short, but technical (and grueling for the uninitiated) climb.**
0.43	2.94	**L**	There is an intersection at the top of the hill. The right trail is marked **"to trailhead."** This is a quick way back to the parking lot if you have run out of daylight or feel that you have gotten in over your head. This is the halfway point for this loop. Turn **left** onto the **Laurel Ridge Trail.**
0.0	2.94		This first section is very fast. There is more than half a mile of undulating hills, which have an overall **downhill slant** to them. This is some of my favorite singletrack riding around. Enjoy!
0.53	3.47	**BR**	You will come to a log crossing followed by a right turn. From this point the longest uphill on the loop begins. It starts at a gradual grade and gets increasingly steeper,
0.43 GPS 8	3.90 180'	**S**	Top of hardest hill on the loop.
0.06	3.96		Shortly before the next downhill there is a left spur, which leads out to the **Claypit Creek Overlook**, where there is a beautiful view of **the Navesink River**, especially in the fall or early spring when there are no leaves on the trees.
0.00	3.96	**S**	The main trail continues and begins a very rugged descent marred with switchbacks and numerous waterbars.
0.49	4.45	**S**	Eventually the trail levels out and continues to rise and fall over a number of smaller hills. Go straight at intersection.
0.30	4.75	**S**	There is one last technical descent characterized by lots of loose rocks.

Pt. to Point	Cume	Turn	Landmark
0.13	4.88	S	The trail dumps you out right into the **dismount area.**
0.03	4.91		Back to parking lot. End of route.
GPS 1	25'		

Rocky Point Loop: This loop starts from the Rocky Point Parking Area. It is short, but very sweet. It can easily be piggy-backed onto either of the other routes to create a long, challenging ride. The Rocky Point Trail was created in the late 1990s to take advantage of the largely undeveloped lands on the portion of Hartshorne nearest the shoreline.

Total route distance: 2.87 miles
Ride time for an *advanced* rider: 0.25–0.75 hours

GPS Waypoints and Elevation Heights:

GPS 9	N40 23.436 W73 59.344	190'
GPS 10	N40 23.162 W73 58.942	55'
GPS 11	N40 23.194 W73 59.236	120'
GPS 12	N40 23.445 W73 59.424	120'
GPS 13	N40 23.548 W73 59.511	160'
GPS 14	N40 23.638 W73 59.373	225'
GPS 9	N40 23.436 W73 59.344	190'

Pt. to Point	Cume	Turn	Landmark
0.00	0.00		From the **information board**, head back to
GPS 9	190'		the other end of the Rocky Point parking lot.
0.05	0.05	R	At parking lot entrance. Pass a metal gate.
0.02	0.07	L	Take first **left** onto the Rocky Point Trail (black diamond). The singletrack trail heads downhill with a few tight turns in the first hundred yards.
0.20	0.27	S	Cross a **small wooden bridge** at the bottom of the hill. During the next section, there are **numerous log crossings.**
0.44	0.71	R	At three-way intersection
0.05	0.76	L	Onto plateau.
0.07	0.83	S	Across paved road. Climb a rooty hill.
GPS 10	55'		

Pt. to Point	Cume	Turn	Landmark
0.11	0.94	S	Pass a **scenic overlook** and start to head back down hill.
0.21 GPS 11	1.17 120'	R	Turn **right** onto paved road and head straight uphill.
0.02	1.19	L	Take first **left** back into woods. Singletrack trail crosses **small wooden bridge** and continues to climb.
0.46	1.65	S	Trail begins **long, steep climb**. Trail switches back to the right and climbs to the top of the hill.
0.09	1.74	S	**Top of hill.**
0.44 GPS 12	2.18 120'	S	Across paved road. Head back into woods. Head up a short, technical climb before the trail levels out and crosses a **small wooden bridge**. Then climb again.
0.23 GPS 13	2.41 160'	S	Cross another paved road.
0.01	2.42	R	Once in the woods, turn **right** and climb on singletrack trail. There is some loose gravel/rock. It is a steep, technical climb.
0.10	2.52	S	**Top of hill.**
0.07 GPS 14	2.59 225'	R	Three right turns in quick succession bring you onto the **Cuesta Ridge Trail** fire road.
0.14	2.73	BL	**Bear left** at fork.
0.01	2.74	L	Onto paved road.
0.06	2.80	R	Back into **Rocky Point parking area.**
0.07 GPS 9	2.87 190'		Back to **information board**. End of route.

Josh Pierce high above Sandy Hook.

Photo by Joe Layton

25. HENRY HUDSON TRAIL

West section

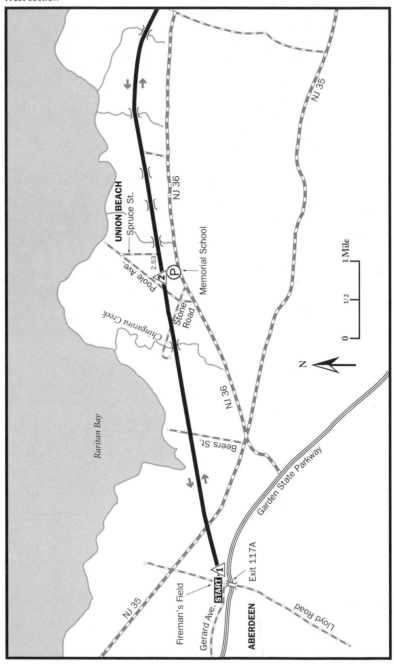

East section

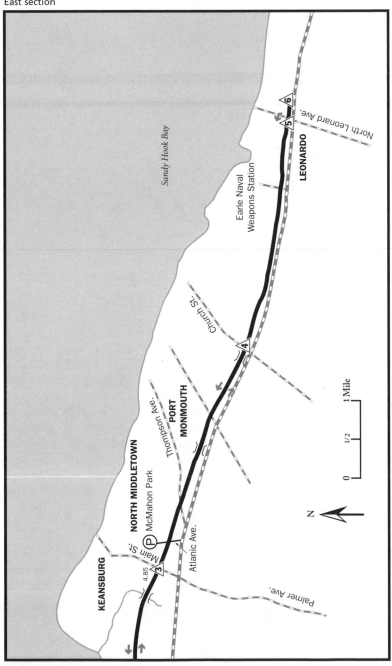

9.60 miles
Aberdeen to Belford, Monmouth Co.

HIGHLIGHTS	**Beginner**
TERRAIN:	**Smooth paved surface**
TOPOGRAPHY:	**Flat grade railbed**
DIFFICULTY:	**Recreational, nontechnical**
TRAIL TYPES:	**Multitrack**

GENERAL INFORMATION

The Henry Hudson Trail is a part of the Monmouth County Park System. For more information, contact:

> Monmouth County Park System
> 805 Newman Springs Road
> Lincroft, NJ 07738
> (908) 842-4000
> www.monmouthcountyparks.com
> info@monmouthcountyparks.com

Directions: The Henry Hudson Trail runs parallel to Route 36 from Aberdeen to Leonardo. There are three off-street parking areas that access the trail. One is at the intersection of Gerard Avenue and Lloyd Road in Aberdeen. Another is at the Memorial School and Scholer Park in Union Beach. The third is at McMahon Park in North Middletown. The route described below begins and ends at the western end of the trail in Aberdeen. These are directions to the Fireman's field parking lot.

Take the Garden State Parkway south to Exit 117A. After passing through the tollbooth, turn left at the first intersection onto Lloyd Road. Cross over the GSP and continue to the first light. The parking lot is just beyond the next traffic light on the left-hand side.

Public Transportation: The Aberdeen-Matawan Train Station is on the North Jersey Coast Line of NJ Transit. From the train station, turn right onto Atlantic Avenue north to the T-intersection with Route 516. Turn right and take Route 516 east across the Garden State Parkway. Take the first right onto Gerard Avenue and follow it to the first light. The trailhead is right off this intersection across the road on the right (GPS 1: N40 25.382 W74 12.702)

Size: 9 miles of trail.

Park Hours: Dawn to dusk, year-round.

Entry Fee: No charge.

Trail Classifications: There is only one trail. It is designated as easiest, or nontechnical.

Trail Maps: There is an information board with a detailed map of the trail about 3 miles from the western end of the trail at the Memorial School. Trail maps are available by mail directly from the Monmouth County Park System.

Restrooms: There are restrooms at McMahon Park at the midway point of the trail.

Nearby Mountain Biking Areas: Cheesequake State Park is 5 miles west of the Henry Hudson Trail. Hartshorne Woods Park is 3 miles east of the eastern end of the trail.

Other Activities: Running, walking, sightseeing, inline skating.

OVERVIEW

The Henry Hudson Trail is fairly new in existence. It has been developed as a multi-use trail. It was designed to give Monmouth County residents a usable fitness area. The trail is also intended to be used as a means for visiting the many historical sites that the trail passes. The trail forms a leg of the New Jersey Coastal Heritage Trail, which extends from its headquarters at Cheesequake State Park all the way down to Cape May.

History: The Henry Hudson Trail is a rail-trail. It was formerly the Central Railroad of New Jersey rail line between Aberdeen and Atlantic Highlands. There are numerous designated points of interest along the trail.

Terrain/Trail Composition: The Henry Hudson trail is extremely flat. As a former railway, the inclines are limited to that which a train could comfortably travel. The entire trail was paved in the fall of 1996. It is uniformly about 8 feet wide, and the surface is smooth enough for inline skates. The only drawback to the trail being paved is that the tendency for broken glass to get on the trail will be more problematic for flats than it was when the trail was hard-packed dirt.

SPECIFIC TRAIL DIRECTIONS

Recreational Spur: This route encompasses the entire Henry Hudson Trail from the parking lot on the corner of Gerard Avenue and Lloyd Road in Aberdeen to the end of the paved trail at North Leonard Avenue in Belford.

The trail is a spur, which is 9 miles long. The directions will only be travelling in one direction. Follow the directions backward to get back to the start from the eastern end of the trail.

The route is pretty easily broken up into smaller sections. If you are looking for a shorter ride than the entire 18 miles, you can either start at the beginning of the route and turn around when you start to get tired, or you can start at one of the other two parking areas in the middle of the trail.

Total route distance: 9.60 miles (one way)
Ride time for a *recreational* rider: 1.0–2.0 hours (one way)

GPS Waypoints and Elevation Heights:

GPS 1	N40 25.382 W74 12.702	35'
GPS 2	N40 26.535 W74 10.367	20'
GPS 3	N40 26.401 W74 07.819	15'
GPS 4	N40 25.421 W74 05.613	15'
GPS 5	N40 24.869 W74 03.452	20'
GPS 6	N40 24.791 W74 03.002	20'

Pt. to Point	Cume	Turn	Landmark
			Starting from the **Fireman's Field** parking lot at the corner of **Gerard Avenue** and **Lloyd Road** in **Aberdeen**, the trailhead is across the street, next to the Shell gas station.
0.00	0.00	S	Enter onto the trail. **The entire trail is paved.**
GSP 1	35'		
0.30	0.30	S	Cross a wooden bridge over the

Pt. to Point	Cume	Turn	Landmark
			Luppatatong Creek.
0.07	0.37	S	Cross bridge over **Route 35.**
0.27	0.64	S	Cross **Beers Street.**
0.19	0.83	S	Across a street. Pass the Marie Catrell playground.
0.08	0.91	S	Across a street. Trail eventually comes out and runs parallel to a street.
0.15	1.06	S	At stop sign by the Cornucopia Restaurant. Cross to the left side of the street.
0.03	1.09	L	Reenter the trail.
0.17	1.26	S	Across a street.
0.16	1.42	S	Across a street.
0.18	1.60	S	Across a wooden bridge over the **Chingorora Creek.**
0.12	1.72	S	Across **Stone Road.**
0.27	1.99	S	Across **Florence.**
0.23	2.22	S	Across **Poole Avenue** Trail runs parallel to a small street for a while. Pass a school.
0.31 GPS 2	2.53 20'		**Memorial School.** There is a large **information board** alongside the trail with a large, detailed map of the Henry Hudson Trail.
0.06	2.59	S	Across **Spruce Street.**
0.11	2.70	S	Across wooden bridge over **Flat Creek.**
0.21	2.91	S	Across **Union Avenue** Pass the Union Beach Memorial Library, Goodies Ice Cream Parlor, and Stevie G's sports bar. The trail runs parallel to Jersey Avenue for a while.
0.22	3.13	S	Across wooden bridge over creek. To the left there is a great view of the **Manhattan skyline** and the **Varazzano Narrows Bridge.**
0.17	3.30	S	Across small wooden bridge over a small creek.
0.14	3.44	S	Across street.
0.10	3.54	S	Across arched wooden bridge over creek.
0.30	3.84	S	Across small wooden bridge over wide creek.
0.12	3.96	S	Across **Central Avenue.** The trail runs

Pt. to Point	Cume	Turn	Landmark
			parallel to 6th Street for a while.
0.21	4.17	S	Across street.
0.32	4.49	S	Across long wooden bridge over wide creek.
0.07	4.56	S	Across **Creek Street.**
0.06	4.62	S	Across **Church Street.**
0.23	4.85	S	Across **Main Street** in **Keansburg.**
GPS 3	15'		**McMahon Park** will be on the left after the intersection. There are basketball courts, softball fields, ice skating rinks, a playground, and restrooms at the park.
0.61	5.46	S	Across **Atlantic Avenue.** Pass several softball fields on the left.
0.16	5.62	S	Across **Thompson Avenue.** The trail runs right next to **Route 36** for the rest of the spur.
0.27	5.89	S	Pass through gate in the thick concrete wall.
0.08	5.97	S	Across small wooden bridge.
0.34	6.31	S	Across road on a diagonal.
0.14	6.45	S	Across **New Street** and **Main Street** in **Port Monmouth.** Pass the Middletown Train Caboose and train station on the left.
0.13	6.58	S	Across street.
0.40	6.98	S	Across wooden bridge over wide creek.
0.11	7.09	S	Across **Church Street.**
GPS 4	15'		
0.19	7.28	S	Across a street.
0.19	7.47	S	Across **East Road.**
0.89	8.36	S	Cross entrance road for **Earle Naval Weapons Station.** Cross under a bridge.
0.09	8.45	S	Cross **Broadway** at traffic light on Route 36.
0.24	8.69	S	Cross **Appleton Avenue** next to the traffic light on Route 36.
0.32	9.01	S	Cross **Thompson Avenue** next to the traffic light on Route 36.
0.09	9.10	S	Cross **North Leonard Avenue.**
GPS 5	20'		
0.40	9.50	S	Pass a parking lot on the right for the **Monmouth County Parks.** There is a restroom with indoor plumbing here.

Pt. to Point	Cume	Turn	Landmark
0.10 GPS 6	9.60 20'	X	The trail ends at Avenue D. End of spur. To get back to Aberdeen, follow the directions in reverse.

A sign proclaiming the existence of the Henry Hudson Trail.

26. HUBER WOODS PARK

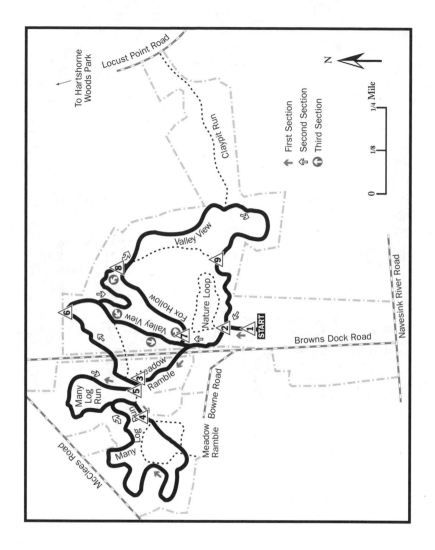

4.25 miles
Locust, Monmouth Co.

HIGHLIGHTS	Beginner – Intermediate
TERRAIN:	Sandy, some roots, logs
TOPOGRAPHY:	Several long climbs, rolling hills
DIFFICULTY:	Moderate to difficult
TRAIL TYPES:	Mainly singletrack

GENERAL INFORMATION

Huber Woods Park is a part of the Monmouth County Park System. For more information, contact:

Monmouth County Park System
805 Newman Springs Road
Lincroft, NJ 07738
(908) 842-4000
www.monmouthcountyparks.com
info@monmouthcountyparks.com

Directions: Huber Woods Park is located in Locust, only a mile or so southwest of Hartshorne Woods Park. Take State Highway 35 to Navesink River Road. Take Navesink River Road 2.8 miles east and turn left onto Brown's Dock Road (a dirt road). The park entrance is at the top of the hill.

Size: 6 miles of trails on 255 acres.

Park Hours: 8 a.m. to dusk, year-round.

Entry Fee: No charge.

Trail Classifications: All trails are marked by a symbol designating its accessibility and the skill level recommended for completion of the trail. All of the trails in all of the Monmouth County Park System share this trail rating system.

Note: The trail rating system is designed for hiking and is not as accurate for biking.

Green Circles indicate highly maintained gradual grade trails designed primarily for walking.

Blue Squares signify multiple-use trails with moderate grades and relatively easy access.

Black Diamonds indicate steep grades, challenging terrain, and minimal maintenance on trails designed for experienced bikers, hikers, and equestrians.

Trail Maps: Trail maps are available at the information center at the head of the trail at the parking lot.

Restrooms: There are public restrooms in the environmental center.

Closest Mountain Biking Area: Hartshorne Woods Park is a mile or so northeast of Huber.

Other Park Activities: Walking, hiking, horseback riding.

OVERVIEW

Huber is very much like a younger sibling to Hartshorne in terms of mountain biking, although it is a substantial size on its own. Huber does not get as crowded with mountain bikes as Hartshorne, but on the other hand, there is not as much of a variety of terrain. As with Hartshorne, there are many different variations of interconnecting loops at Huber. My advise is to explore and come up with your own ride.

History: Huber Woods Park was established in 1974. The original Huber home, built in 1927, is now an environmental center. There is also an equestrian program center down the hill from the environmental center.

Terrain/Trail Composition: The terrain at Huber is very similar to that at Hartshorne. Overall, the trails are fast and dry in comparison to other New Jersey areas. The ground is very smooth, and there is a noticeable lack of exposed rock. The woods in this area are dense and deep green. There are a plethora of fallen trees across many of the trails. Most are rideable, depending on your ability level.

There are any number of combinations of trails to ride at Huber. Like all of the parks in the Monmouth County Park System, Huber uses a system for rating the difficulty of its trails that borrows its symbols from the world of alpine skiing. Circles demarcate easier trails. Moderate trails are squares and the most challenging ones are diamonds.

Linking Huber & Hartshorne On Bike: Hartshorne and Huber are less than 2 miles apart at their closest points, and linking the 2 parks by bike can amount to a daylong mountain bike adventure less than 5 miles form the Jersey Shore. From the trails at Huber, take Claypit Run out to Locust Point Road and turn left. Take the first right onto Locust Avenue and cross the bridge over the Navesink River. Turn right at the five-way intersection onto Navesink Avenue and take an immediate right onto Hartshorne Road. In less than half a mile there is a trailhead on the left side of the road. Take this trail up until it intersects with the Laurel Ridge Trail in the Hartshorne Woods trail system. If you turn left onto the Laurel Ridge Trail you will come to the Buttermilk Valley parking area and information board within half a mile.

SPECIFIC TRAIL DIRECTIONS

Intermediate Loop: Huber Woods is a lot like Hartshorne. The hills are generally not as big or long as those at Hartshorne and there tend to be many more log obstacles. The biggest difference between the 2 parks is that Huber is very equestrian-friendly. Most likely, you will run into horses at Huber. There is an equestrian riding center at Huber, and horses are allowed on every trail that mountain bikes are allowed to use. This loop is a little more than 4 miles long and covers more than half of the trail-miles at Huber. Almost the entire route is singletrack.

Total route distance: 4.25 miles
Ride time for an *intermediate* rider: 0.75–1.25 hours

GPS Waypoints and Elevation Heights:

GPS 1	N40 23.165	W74 02.044	150'
GPS 2	N40 23.215	W74 02.093	150'
GPS 3	N40 23.412	W74 02.367	135'
GPS 4	N40 23.428	W74 02.406	105'
GPS 5	N40 23.405	W74 02.319	135'
GPS 6	N40 23.604	W74 02.084	125'
GPS 7	N40 23.322	W74 02.152	130'
GPS 8	N40 23.480	W74 01.953	50'
GPS 9	N40 23.270	W74 01.889	135'

Pt. to Point	Cume	Turn	Landmark
0.00 GPS 1	0.00 150'	S	From parking lot at information center, take thin trail straight across the field to the trailhead.
0.06 GPS 2	0.06 150'	L	Onto **Fox Hollow Trail**. Winding singletrack.
0.17	0.23	L	Turn **left** at fork onto **Meadow Ramble**.
0.02	0.25	S	Across **Fire Road**. Stay on singletrack.
0.03	0.28	S	Across maintained dirt road. Stay on singletrack. Trail starts to climb.
0.16	0.44	L	Stay on **Meadow Ramble** Trail.
0.02 GPS 3	0.46 135'	R	At first entrance to **Many Log Run**.
0.53 GPS 4	0.99 100'	L	At three-way intersection. Climb up loose, technical hill.
0.05	1.04	T/R	At T-intersection onto wider trail. Follow directions on trail marker for blue square trail.
0.08	1.12	S	Come into meadow clearing. Head straight across to other side.
0.04	1.16	S	Back into the woods on the other side of the clearing.
0.07	1.23	R	Take the **right** fork.
0.04	1.27	S	Take the middle of three branches (**Many Log Run, black diamond**). The trail becomes twisty singletrack with lots of aged, crumbling log crossings.
0.78 GPS 5	2.05 100'	L	At fork onto the bottom half of the **Many Log Run**.
0.54	2.59	L	Onto wider trail.
0.02	2.61	BL	Stay on wider trail.
0.04 GPS 5	2.65 135'	BL	At clearing. Stay on the singletrack route on the edge of the meadow.
0.11	2.76	S	Across maintained dirt road on a diagonal. Get back on singletrack on the other side.
0.17	2.93	BR	At fork after large, built up log pile.
0.06 GPS 6	2.99 125'	R	To avoid a technical, rutted downhill with numerous waterbars (**Valley View, blue square**).

Pt. to Point	Cume	Turn	Landmark
0.02	3.01	L	At four-way intersection onto **Fox Hollow**.
GPS 7	130'		This section is downhill.
0.28	3.29	R	At three-way intersection onto singletrack
GPS 8	50'		(**Valley View, black diamond**).
0.38	3.67	R	At three-way intersection. Post sign says, "To Trailhead."
0.27	3.94	BL	Stay on trail as it bears left and **Fox Hollow**
GPS 9	135'		comes in from the right.
0.25	4.19	L	At the trailhead intersection by the parking
GPS 2	150'		lot. Ride across field on singletrack.
0.06	4.25		Back to parking lot by information center.
GPS 1	150'		End of route.

The information board at Huber Woods Park.

Photo by Joshua M. Pierce

27. RINGWOOD STATE PARK

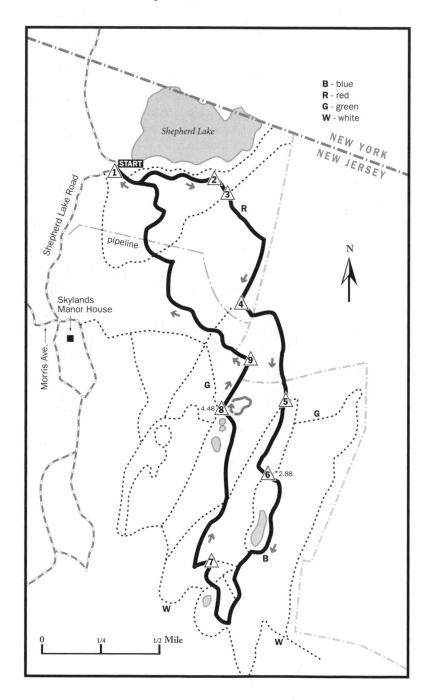

B - blue
R - red
G - green
W - white

Shepherd Lake

NEW YORK
NEW JERSEY

START

Shepherd Lake Road

pipeline

Skylands
Manor House

Morris Ave.

N

R

G

G

4.48

2.88

B

W

W

0   1/4   1/2 Mile

6.55 miles
Ringwood, Passaic Co.

HIGHLIGHTS	Moderate – Difficult
TERRAIN:	Extremely rocky in sections, fairly rocky everywhere
TOPOGRAPHY:	Very hilly, almost mountainous Lots of long, extended climbs
DIFFICULTY:	Intermediate to technically and aerobically advanced
TRAIL TYPES:	Lots of technical fire road, innumerable singletrack trails

GENERAL INFORMATION

Ringwood State Park is a part of the New Jersey Division of Parks and Forestry. For more information, contact:

Ringwood State Park
1304 Sloatsburg Road
Ringwood, NJ 07456
(973) 962-7031
www.state.nj.us/dep/parksandforests/parks/ringwood.html

Directions: Take Interstate 287 north into New York State. Continue north on I-87. Take one of the first exits: Exit 15A for Route 17 north. Turn left at the light at the end of the ramp and stay on the road for 1.5 miles. Take the first exit for Sloatsburg Road and continue for 4 miles. Turn left into the park at the Skylands/Shepherd Lake entrance (Morris Road) and take the road to the top of the hill. Turn left at the four-way intersection onto a level road and follow it to the Shepherd Lake tollbooth. Park in the parking lot up the hill to the left.

Size: More than 30 miles of trails on 4,034 acres.

Park Hours: Dawn to dusk, year-round.

Entry Fee: Fees are charged from Memorial Day to Labor Day for parking at the Shepherd Lake, Ringwood, and Skyland sections of the park. Shepherd Lake is a popular destination for busloads of swimmers during the summer. The New Jersey State Park Pass costs $35 and is good for a year. It gives you unlimited access to any of the state parks (Cheesequake, Allaire, Round Valley, Sandy Hook). Daily fees at Shepherds Lake are $5 per car weekdays and $10 per car weekends and holidays.

Trail Classifications: None of the trails at Ringwood are marked for difficulty. There are 10 color-coded, marked trails, of which 3 are marked for multiple use (the rest are off limits to bikes). In addition, there are numerous unmarked, unmaintained trails.

Trail Maps: Trail maps can be obtained at the bathhouse at Shepherd Lake.

Restrooms: Restrooms are located in the bathhouse at Shepherd Lake.

Nearby Mountain Biking Areas: Wawayanda State Park is about 10–15 miles west of the western end of Ringwood.

Other Park Activities: Hiking, swimming, boating, hunting, shooting, fishing, picnicking, cross-country skiing, and snowmobiling are all popular activities at Ringwood.

OVERVIEW

Ringwood is a large state park that contains countless miles of great off-road riding. The park is situated on more than 4,000 acres of land, and there are trails running over it in every conceivable direction. The park is bordered to the south by Ramapo State Forest.

Beyond the sheer size of Ringwood, there is also an element of vastness that you do not find at most of the mountain biking areas so close to New York City. As opposed to Hartshorne, Mercer, or Lewis Morris, Ringwood is not surrounded on all sides by suburban sprawl. Virtually none of the borders of the park are roads, or even back streets. I have gotten lost in Ringwood and been unable to find a paved road until I was 5–10 miles outside the park boundary—unfortunately, that road was Route 17, about a 20-mile road ride back to the Shepherd's Lake parking lot. Ringwood is the closest thing to wilderness that New York metro area has to offer.

Terrain/Trail Composition: If you come from the southern part of the state, the first thing you will notice when you begin to ride Ringwood is its rockiness. Compared to most of the parks in Central Jersey, Ringwood is full of rocky terrain and littered with rock gardens. The next thing you will notice is that the climbs go on and on. Ringwood is part of the same range of mountains that cover the northwestern region of the state and give the state alpine skiing and snowboarding farther west.

Ringwood is divided by a rocky pipeline fire road and is riddled with numerous other fire roads, which crisscross each other throughout the park. In general, the pipeline is not navigable by anything other than serious four-wheel-drives and quads, which you may encounter occasionally. From the relatively stable fire roads emanate a whole slew of singletrack trails that twist and turn their way throughout the park.

History: Ringwood became the property of Abram S. Hewitt in the mid-1800s after producing many essential items for the colonies during the American Revolution. In 1936, the original property of the Ringwood Manor House and its surrounding 95 acres were deeded to the State of New Jersey. Since then the state has added much of the remaining acreage to the park under the Green Acres program, including the 1966 acquisition of the Skyland Manor estate.

Skyland Manor, built by Clarence MacKenzie Lewis in the 1920s as a summer house, has been maintained as a fine example of an English Jacobean mansion. Ringwood Manor House remains an accurate depiction of Hewitt's life in the late nineteenth and early twentieth centuries. It is a National Historic Landmark.

SPECIFIC TRAIL DIRECTIONS
Advanced Loop: This route combines fire road and technical multitrack riding with a lot of great singletrack. Ringwood is a very hilly, almost mountainous area. The trails are very strenuous. This route includes most of the highlights of the park.

Total route distance: 6.55 miles
Ride guide for *advanced* rider: 1.0–1.75 hours

GPS Waypoints and Elevation in feet:

GPS 1	N41 08.114 W74 13.909	640'
GPS 2	N41 08.152 W74 13.247	650'
GPS 3	N41 08.160 W74 13.134	825'
GPS 4	N41 07.680 W74 13.245	680'
GPS 5	N41 07.260 W74 13.269	805'
GPS 6	N41 06.932 W74 13.514	815'
GPS 7	N41 06.629 W74 13.794	890'
GPS 8	N41 07.209 W74 13.646	700'
GPS 9	N41 07.399 W74 13.489	715'

Pt. to Point	Cume	Turn	Landmark
0.0 GPS 1	0.0 640'	S	This route starts at the parking lot just inside the **Shepherd's Lake** tollbooth and to the east by the boathouse. Get on the **Red Trail** fire road and head straight.
0.70 GPS 2	0.70 650'	R	Climb up hill at intersection heading away from the end of the lake. Doubletrack trail is steep, with lots of loose rocks.
0.13 GPS 3	0.83 805'	S	At intersection after the trail levels out. Trail becomes singletrack.
0.58 GPS 4	1.41 680'	L	Switchback turn near bottom of *steep downhill*.
0.07	1.48	R	The trail levels out.
0.13	1.61	R	Stay to the right and head up **loose, rocky climb**. The first part of the climb is very steep, but then becomes a longer, more gradual climb.
0.10	1.71	R	Onto singletrack climb, which then levels out and becomes multi-track.
0.09	1.80	S	**Short, rocky climb.**
0.20	2.00	S	Becomes singletrack again.
0.10	2.10	S	**Really rocky, technical section.**
0.08	2.18	S	At intersection. Cross wider trail. Stay on singletrack.
0.04	2.22	S	Rocky, technical, serpentine climb— gradual pitch.
0.15 GPS 5	2.37 805'	S	At intersection. Cross wide-open **pipeline road**. Stay on singletrack.

Pt. to Point	Cume	Turn	Landmark
0.07	2.44	**BR**	Onto wider fire road.
0.07	2.51	**BL**	Take the left fork that heads up long, gradual fire road climb.
0.37 GPS 6	2.88 815'	**L**	At three-way intersection.
0.05	2.93	**R**	At three-way intersection. Trail is still fire road and becomes **fast downhill.**
0.35	3.28	**L**	**Bear left** and then take **immediate left** onto wide singletrack into deeper woods.
0.19	3.47	**S**	Ride straight across fire road. Stay on singletrack. Trail becomes a *steep, twisty, technical downhill.* Stay on singletrack.
0.09	3.56	**S**	Trail gradually begins long climb.
0.09 GPS 7	3.65 890'	**T/L**	At top of hill onto level fire road at T-intersection. Quickly becomes *long, fast downhill.*
0.39	4.04	**S**	At intersection. *Watch for water channels.*
0.44 GPS 8	4.48 700'	**R**	Onto wide, level dirt road at T-intersection. This is the **White/Green Dot Trail.**
0.15	4.63	**L**	Take the **left fork** after passing through the gate of a **nineteenth-century stone manor.**
0.16 GPS 9	4.79 715'	**L**	Onto **long, steep granny gear climb.** Trail is singletrack with numerous rocky sections. There are 3 tight switchback turns climbing up the hill.
0.14	4.93	**S**	Top of hill. Trail becomes singletrack.
0.10	5.03	**S**	At intersection across pipeline road. Stay on singletrack.
0.17	5.20	**S**	At intersection across wider trail. Stay on singletrack.
0.57	5.77	**S**	At intersection across thin doubletrack. Stay on singletrack.
0.08	5.85	**R**	Stay on trail as it twists around to the right.
0.54	6.39	**L**	Onto original boathouse fire road. Lake will be to your right.
0.16 GPS 1	6.55 640'		Back to parking lot. End of route.

28. WASHINGTON VALLEY PARK (CHIMNEY ROCK PARK)

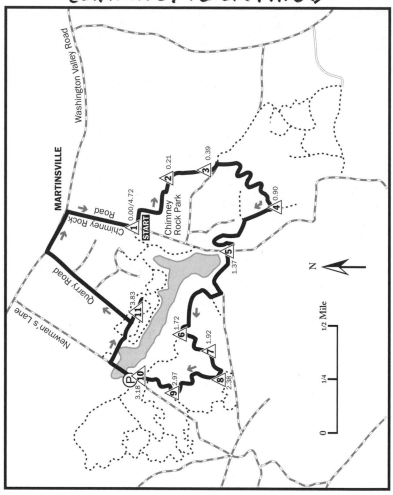

4.80/4.72 miles
Martinsville, Somerset Co.

HIGHLIGHTS	**Intermediate – Very Advanced**
TERRAIN:	Relatively smooth to very rocky
TOPOGRAPHY:	Several longer hills, some
	flatter twisty sections
DIFFICULTY:	Moderate to extremely difficult
TRAIL TYPES:	Lots of twisty singletrack, limited
	fire road

GENERAL INFORMATION
Washington Valley Park is a part of the Somerset County Parks Commission. For more information, contact:

Somerset County Parks Commission
PO Box 5327
North Branch, NJ 08876
(908) 722-1200
www.somersetcountyparks.org
prangers@scparks.org

Directions: Take I-287 to Route 22 East. Pass the first exit for Chimney Rock Road. Turn right at the second exit (0.6 miles) for Thompson Avenue/Bound Brook/Martinsville. Immediately, take the jug handle to the right for Martinsville and cross over Route 22. Turn left at the stop sign onto Route 525 north. Follow the road as it winds its way up through a gorge. After the road levels out, Chimney Rock Park will be on the right. Park here for the grand tour loop.

For the western route (and the heart of the mountain biking) continue past the park and turn left at the T-intersection. Turn left onto Newman's Lane in half a mile. Take Newman's Lane down and across a narrow bridge. The parking lot is on the left side just as the road starts to head up the long, steep hill.

Size: 15 to 20 miles of trails on 1,500 to 2,000 acres.

Park Hours: Dawn to dusk, year-round.

Entry Fee: No charge.

Trail Classifications: The Somerset County Parks Commission has no classification system of its own for the park. The western section contains sections of roller-coaster-esque, smooth singletrack as well as very technical, rocky, twisting singletrack with an excessive number of loose-rock sections. The eastern section contains longer, steeper, grinding climbs and descents, with even more loose rocky sections thrown in for good measure. The trails between Newman's Lane and Chimney Rock Road along the reservoir are smoother and less hilly.

Trail Maps: There is a generic map on display at the information board in the parking lot on Newman's Lane. There is a dispenser for trail maps at the information board.

Restrooms: There is a portable toilet in the Chimney Rock Park parking lot on Chimney Rock Road.

Nearby Mountain Biking Areas: Sourland Mountain Preserve is about 15 miles south. Round Valley is about 15 miles west. The Delaware & Raritan Canal State Park comes within 10 miles of Washington Valley Park to the south. Six Mile Run is about 15 miles south.

Other Park Activities: Hiking, fishing, baseball, basketball, snowmobiling, and cross-country skiing.

OVERVIEW

The riding at Washington Valley Park surrounds Chimney Rock Park, which is a small, outdoor, port-based park on Chimney Rock Road in Martinsville. This park acts as a hub, from which singletrack trails extend in several directions. The main base for Washington Valley Park is the parking lot on Newman's Lane. From what originally started as parking for 2–3 cars, the new lot (with 20–30 parking spots) is routinely filled on busy summer weekends.

Terrain/Trail Composition: The terrain at White Rock is very rocky. Where there are hills (the eastern and western sections), the hills are big and long, and excessively rocky. The central connecting section of the park between Newman's Lane and Chimney Rock Road is less rocky and less hilly, but there are still patches of rocky terrain and short, but steep hills.

The trails are almost entirely singletrack, rocky and extremely twisty in nature. There are numerous sections where the trail will take a tight 270-degree turn before heading off in a completely different direction. The park trail system has matured greatly over the past 10 years, changing in nature from tight, twisty, narrow, fresh singletrack trails to wider, more heavily traveled, increasingly rocky trails. The trails are still a lot of fun— in fact, Washington Valley Park is one of the most popular places to ride a mountain bike in New Jersey.

The trails off Newman's Lane were all cut in the mid-1990s. They were rocky and technical, but there was still a layer of topsoil on the trails, which made them smoother. Today, the topsoil is long gone. The trails are made up in large sections of jagged, exposed rock. The bike of choice has changed along with the trail composition, and most mountain bikers here today are riding cross-country full suspension and free-ride bikes.

History: White Rock is a fairly new area for mountain biking. Trails began to show up all over the park at about the same time that I first found out that bikes were allowed on the trails in the spring of 1995. There is not much of a history to the park. The western section borders an active rock quarrying operation, and there are several trails that wind back and forth across the remnants of a few ancient stone boundary walls.

SPECIFIC TRAIL DIRECTIONS
This route is a good introduction to the riding available at Washington Valley Park. It encompasses all of the sections of the park and the highlights of the most technical aspects of White Rock. At less than 5 miles, it is deceptively long. The loop covers a lot of ground, and it feels like a much longer route than the mileage would have you believe.

Advanced Western Loop: : This loop starts and ends at the Chimney Rock Park parking lot. It is a deceptively long ride, even at less than 5 miles. This loop encompasses all of the sections of the park: the Eastern White Rock section, the Western section and all of the intermediary sections between Chimney Rock Road and Newman's Lane. This is an advanced loop, which tends to become abusive in spots.

Total route distance: 4.72 miles
Ride time for an *advanced* rider: 2.0–3.0 hours

GPS Waypoints and Elevation Heights:

GPS 1	N40 35.666 W74 33.587	210'
GPS 2	N40 35.577 W74 33.406	170'
GPS 3	N40 35.462 W74 33.358	155'
GPS 4	N40 35.170 W74 33.561	290'
GPS 5	N40 35.345 W74 33.812	155'
GPS 6	N40 35.557 W74 33.967	160'
GPS 7	N40 35.458 W74 34.133	320'
GPS 8	N40 35.388 W74 34.460	355'
GPS 9	N40 35.672 W74 34.413	265'
GPS 10	N40 35.773 W74 34.428	220'
GPS 11	N40 35.650 W74 33.914	225'

Pt. to Point	Cume	Turn	Landmark
0.00 GPS 1	0.00 210'		From the back of the parking lot at the information board, ride down a paved path to the right between the last softball field and the tennis courts, away from **Chimney Rock Road.**
0.08	0.08	S	At the end of the pavement onto grass. Head toward the far right corner of the open field.
0.21 GPS 2	0.21 170'	S	Head into the woods. Ride **downhill** next to the stairs and cross an **arched wooden bridge** over a small creek.
0.04	0.25	R	On the other side of the bridge.
0.08	0.33	R	At a fork. The trail winds its way to a **very technical, tricky stream crossing** and up a nasty little off-camber, rooty climb to a paved road.
0.06 GPS 3	0.39 155'	L	Onto **Gilbride Road.**
0.01	0.40	R	At first opportunity (before crossing the bridge). Start a *long, extremely rocky climb* with a handful of tricky switchbacks.
0.28	0.68	L	At fork once the trail starts to level out.
0.22 GPS 4	0.90 290'	T/R	At T-intersection. Continue uphill a little bit longer on singletrack.
0.13	1.03	T/L	At T-intersection on flat trail. Trail starts

Pt. to Point	Cume	Turn	Landmark
			down a *steep, rocky downhill.* There are *two tricky switchbacks with lots of loose rocks.*
0.30	1.33	L	At the bottom of the hill onto Chimney Rock Road. Cross bridge.
0.04 GPS 5	1.37 155'	R	Ride through a gate off road just after the bridge. The trail climbs a hill next to the reservoir spillway before leveling off and continuing along the edge of the reservoir.
0.21	1.58	R	Onto a singletrack trail that heads off to the **right** through a break in the chain-link fence. The trail heads downhill before climbing along the edge of the reservoir.
0.14 GPS 6	1.72 160'	L	At three-way intersection. Begin a gradual uphill climb that gets steeper and rockier.
0.10	1.82	R	Onto flatter trail.
0.02	1.84	L	At fork.
0.07	1.91	R	At fork.
0.01 GPS 7	1.92 320'	L	Up short, **steep rock face** at three-way intersection.
0.14	2.06	BR	Onto wider gravel trail.
0.03	2.09	S	Follow trail around (or over) two gigantic boulders. Trail becomes wide gravel road that goes straight past quarry private property.
0.18 GPS 8	2.38 355'	R	Onto relatively smooth singletrack trail into the woods. Cross several log piles.
0.10	2.48	BR	Trail starts to head downhill.
0.04	2.52	L	At three-way intersection. Trail becomes *extremely rocky.* There are numerous log crossings.
0.21	2.73	S	Cross rock bridge over stream. Trail heads downhill.
0.24 GPS 9	2.97 265'	T/R	At T-intersection. Continue downhill toward the parking lot.
0.13	3.10	T/L	At T-intersection at the bottom of the hill onto flat trail.
0.08 GPS 10	3.18 220'	R	Information board at Newman's Lane parking lot. Head down crushed cinder/gravel path

Pt. to Point	Cume	Turn	Landmark
			behind information board.
0.06	3.24	S	Cross big arched wooden footbridge.
0.06	3.30	T/R	At T-intersection. Trail gets narrower, but still flat.
0.07	3.37	L	After rocky stream crossing at three-way intersection into the woods.
0.01	3.38	R	Up hill at first available intersection onto **White Circle** singletrack trail.
0.03	3.41	S	Up hill. Trail becomes the **Red Circle** singletrack trail.
0.11	3.52	S	At four-way intersection. Trail becomes **White Circle** once again.
0.31 GPS 11	3.83 225'	R/L	Turn **right** at a fork and then **left** as a trail feeds in from the right.
0.40	4.23	R	Cross a long, low, wooden boardwalk bridge over a wide marshy area.
0.06	4.29	T/L	At T-intersection at the top of a small hill onto a flat gravel trail along the back end of a handful of residential properties.
0.11	4.40	R	Trail turns **right** and climbs between two houses up to paved road.
0.07	4.47	R	Onto **Chimney Rock Road.**
0.07	4.54	L	Into the **Chimney Rock Park** parking lot.
0.18 GPS 1	4.72 210'		Back to information board. End of route.

Photo by Jeremiah Pierce

Josh Pierce rides through an overgrown field at Washington Valley Park.

29. WAWAYANDA STATE PARK

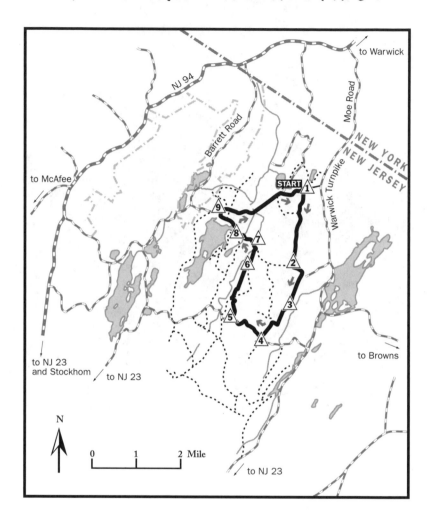

9.43 miles
Hewitt, Passaic Co.

HIGHLIGHTS	Moderate – Extremely Difficult
TERRAIN:	Rocky, technical, muddy in spots
TOPOGRAPHY:	Hilly, with extended climbs
DIFFICULTY:	Hybrid-friendly to difficult
TRAIL TYPES:	Mainly singletrack, some gravel and dirt roads

GENERAL INFORMATION

Wawayanda State Park is a part of the Monmouth County Park System. For more information, contact:

New Jersey Department of Environmental Protection
885 Warwick Turnpike
Hewitt, NJ 07421
(973) 853-4462
www.state.nj.us/dep/parksandforests/parks/wawayanda.html

Directions: From Route 94, 3 miles southwest of Warwick, New York (just south of a Ford dealership), take Moe Road (County Route 21) south for 3.1 miles. The park entrance is on the right. Take the first right turn inside the park to go to the park office. Park in the parking lot. The described route begins at the information board outside the office.

Size: 40 miles of trails on 18,235 acres.

Park Hours: 5 a.m. to 9 p.m., year-round.

Entry Fee: Entrance fees are $5 on weekdays and $10 on weekends between Memorial Day and Labor Day. There is no charge for those walking or on bicycles.

Trail Classifications: There is no trail classification system at Wawayanda. While mountain biking is allowed in most of the park, the trails are not designed for bikes, and there are some where bicycles are off limits, like the 20 miles of Appalachian Trail that run through the northern portion of the park.

Trail Maps: There is a large trail map and information board at the park office just inside the eastern edge of the park by the main park entrance on the Warwick Turnpike (Moe Road).

Restrooms: There are restroom facilities at the park office by the Moe Road entrance and at the main beach area of Lake Wawayanda.

Closest Mountain Biking Area: Diablo Mountain Bike Park at Mountain Creek is about only 5 miles from Wawayanda, but it is a 20-mile drive. Ringwood State Park is about 15 miles to the east.

Other Park Activities: Swimming in Wawayanda Lake, fishing, canoeing, paddling, sailing, hiking, picnicking, and camping are all popular at Wawayanda. In the winter, cross-country skiing, snowshoeing, ice skating, ice fishing, and snowmobiling are common.

OVERVIEW
A rough derivation of *wawayanda* used by the Lenape Indians to mean "water of the mountain." Wawayanda State Park, in Sussex County, is big-scale wilderness about 40 miles as the crow flies from New York City. The 9.43-mile detailed loop takes you through the heart of the 2,167-acre Wawayanda Swamp Natural Area, home to a rare Atlantic White Cedar swamp.

History: Looking back 300 million years, the land that now makes up Wawayanda was close to 30,000 feet above sea level. The tallest mountain range in the world at the time has endured a long decline. Millions of years of erosion, glacial movement, and tectonic shifts have relocated most of the rock of the former peaks all the way across Pennsylvania as far as Lake Erie.

Wawayanda was completely denuded of trees at least twice between the 1860s and the mid-twentieth century to fuel the charcoal blast iron furnace (the remnants of which can still be seen near the shores of Lake Wawayanda). The timber on the land was still being commercially harvested until the 1960s, when Wawayanda State Park was purchased with Green Acres funds and opened to the public.

Terrain/Trail Composition: Overall, the terrain at Wawayanda is rocky and wet in comparison to other New Jersey areas. The Wawayanda plateau is one of the only places in New Jersey where granite bedrock is exposed. Through millions of years of erosion, the granite has been broken up and strewn throughout the area. Also, the bedrock tends to hold water, and there are numerous swampy areas throughout the park.

SPECIFIC TRAIL DIRECTIONS

Advanced Loop: This route starts at the park office just inside the main park entrance off the Warwick Turnpike (Moe Road). It follows rocky singletrack trails straight through the heart of the Wawayanda Swamp Natural Area before joining the Cherry Ridge gravel road. The loop then heads back north on the Red Dot Trail through the natural area before leading to the archaeological remains of the nineteenth-century Double Pond industrial village and 255-acre Lake Wawayanda. From the northern shores of the lake the loop returns to the start by way of paved park roads.

Total route distance: 9.43 miles
Ride time for an *advanced* rider: 1.0–2.0 hours

GPS Waypoints and Elevation Heights:

GPS 1	N41 11.876 W74 23.850	1,245'
GPS 2	N41 10.615 W74 24.168	1,235'
GPS 3	N41 09.932 W74 24.185	1,205'
GPS 4	N41 09.423 W74 24.861	1,300'
GPS 5	N41 09.727 W74 25.474	1,280'
GPS 6	N41 10.620 W74 25.111	1,260'
GPS 7	N41 10.942 W74 24.959	1,205'
GPS 8	N41 11.095 W74 25.313	1,175'
GPS 9	N41 11.564 W74 25.737	1,165'

Pt. to Point	Cume	Turn	Landmark
0.00 GPS 1	0.00 1,245'		Take the paved sidewalk on the left side of the information board down to the park entrance road.
0.01	0.01	R	Onto the paved road.
0.03	0.04	L	**William Hoeferlien trailhead** (blue blaze). Follow the singletrack trail headed into the woods. Begin a long, gradual, rocky, rideable climb.
0.52	0.56	L	At three-way intersection with the **Black Eagle Trail.**

Pt. to Point	Cume	Turn	Landmark
1.12 GPS 2	1.68 1,235'	T/L	At T-intersection. Trail becomes a gravel road and heads into civilization.
0.40	2.08	T/R	At T-intersection where road becomes paved onto the singletrack **Bunker Trail** (yellow blaze). Trail starts out as an overgrown singletrack along a fence and pond, then crosses a long wooden planking footbridge.
0.11	2.19	R	At the Bunker Trail sign. Climb a tiny rooty hill.
0.01	2.20	L	At three-way intersection to get back to the **yellow blaze trail**. Trail becomes smoother and easier to navigate.
0.55 GPS 3	2.75 1,205'	R	At three-way intersection to stay on the yellow-blazed trail. Start a gradual climb.
0.21	2.96	S	Trail begins a *steep, technical descent.*
0.28	3.24	R	At a three-way intersection. Follow the yellow-blazed trail onto a wider dirt trail that winds its way through the woods for a while before climbing to an intersection.
0.56 GPS 4	3.80 1,300'	T/R	At a T-intersection onto **Cherry Ridge Road**—a gravel road that climbs a hill and then back down the other side.
0.47	4.27	S	Pass a **red metal gate**, then a rocky stream crossing.
0.32 GPS 5	4.59 1,280'	R	Onto the **Red Dot Trail** (red blaze) at the trailhead sign at the top of the hill. Then ride downhill to the edge of a pond.
0.34	4.93	R	At a fork onto a nasty, swampy, muddy bog section with numerous primitive log and rock bridges. Eventually, the trail dries and gets smooth and fast.
0.33	5.26	L	At fork. Trail gets rocky.
0.73 GPS 6	5.99 1,260'	T/L	At T-intersection onto a wider trail to stay on the Red Dot Trail.
0.32	6.31	S	Cross a wooden bridge.
0.09 GPS 7	6.40 1,205'	T/L	At T-intersection at the end of the Red Dot Trail. Turn **left** onto **Double Pond Trail** (yellow blaze). Cross a wooden bridge and

Pt. to Point	Cume	Turn	Landmark
			planking before the trail turns **right** and starts a loose, rocky climb.
0.23	6.63	S	Pass a metal gate and then emerge from the woods at a campground. Follow the gravel road through the campground and out to a clearing.
0.14 GPS 8	6.77 1,175'	BR	At a four-way intersection with a gravel road. Take the trail that leads just to the left of the **Historic Iron Furnace.**
0.09	6.86	S	Cross a bridge over stone ruins. Climb to the northeast corner of **Lake Wawayanda.**
0.09	6.95	S	At a three-way intersection past a trail that crosses a dam at the edge of the lake. Follow the gravel road along the north shore of the lake.
0.19	7.14	S	Hug the shoreline and pass a wooden house.
0.20	7.34	R	Onto a paved road into a parking lot. Head straight out across the parking lot.
0.07	7.41	L	Onto a paved road.
0.18 GPS 9	7.59 1,165'	T/R	At T-intersection onto **Wawayanda Road**. The rest of the route is a paved-road ride back to the park office.
1.76	9.35	S	Pass the tollbooths.
0.06	9.41	L	Across the road and up the paved sidewalk.
0.02 GPS 1	9.43 1,245'	X	Back to information board. End of route.

Eelgrass filters the afternoon sun at Wawayanda State Park.

OTHER NOTABLE TRAILS

Babcock Preserve, Greenwich, CT

Directions: Hutchinson Parkway North to Merritt Parkway. Take North Street Exit. Proceed north on North Street about 1.5 miles to a gravel road on the left.

Description: Babcock offers approximately 6 miles of trails, most of which are intermediate with only short hills. There are logs to hop over and rock gardens on the red trail, but otherwise it is a good destination for beginners. There is a map at the trailhead.

The yellow trail is the main one, which loops with other trails branching off from it.

Stewart Airport Buffer Lands, Newburgh, NY

Directions: Interstate 87 (NY Thruway) to Exit 17 to Stewart Airport. You may need a permit, which you can obtain at the NYS Department of Environmental Conservation at the NYS Department of Transportation building at the airport. Travel west from the airport on Route 207 to the parking area on the right.

Description: This is a 6,000-acre parcel of land with lots of old dirt roads good for intermediate riders. The buffer zone is quiet countryside that abounds with wildlife. Interconnecting singletrack is technical with some steep climbs. It's best to avoid this park during hunting season (late October-March) as it is a popular hunting destination—and unlike Westchester, guns are permitted in Putnam county.

Photo by William Schmitt

Navigating an S-turn on an autumn day in Connecticut.

Author Joel D. Sendek has been seeking out mountain-biking destinations in the New York metropolitan area since 1988.